GIDS Analysis

edited by | herausgegeben von

Stefan Bayer
Burkhard Meißner
Matthias Rogg
Gary Schaal
Jörn Thießen

Volume 4 | Band 4

Mathias Voss

Defence in a Changing World

How Defensive Should (NATO) Defence Be?

GERMAN INSTITUTE
FOR DEFENCE AND
STRATEGIC STUDIES

The Deutsche Nationalbibliothek lists this publication in the
Deutsche Nationalbibliografie; detailed bibliographic data
are available on the Internet at http://dnb.d-nb.de
ISBN   978-3-8487-7942-0 (Print)
        978-3-7489-2327-5 (ePDF)

British Library Cataloguing-in-Publication Data
A catalogue record for this book is available from the British Library.
ISBN   978-3-8487-7942-0 (Print)
        978-3-7489-2327-5 (ePDF)

Library of Congress Cataloging-in-Publication Data
Voss, Mathias
Defence in a Changing World
How Defensive Should (NATO) Defence Be?
Mathias Voss
111 pp.
Includes bibliographic references.
ISBN   978-3-8487-7942-0 (Print)
        978-3-7489-2327-5 (ePDF)

Onlineversion
Nomos eLibrary

1st Edition 2021
© Nomos Verlagsgesellschaft, Baden-Baden, Germany 2021. Overall responsibility
for manufacturing (printing and production) lies with Nomos Verlagsgesellschaft mbH
& Co. KG.

Table of Content

1 Introduction

What is defence? In many areas of daily life people discuss what defence is and how to conduct it best. Is 'attack the best defence' as the saying claims? In sports, is the fore-checking of the forwards in hockey or (European) football part of defence? Is the whole team in defence when the opponent is in possession of the ball as in American football—and how can a quarterback sack be called a defensive action? Would that be the equivalent of a defensive army repelling an attack outside of their own country?[1]

The definitions of the word 'defence' found in dictionaries are not very conclusive, either. The Oxford Dictionary for example provides explanations for defence such as: "the action of defending from or resisting attack", "a means of protecting something from attack", or "military measures or resources for protecting a country".[2] Merriam-Webster offers the following definition for the verb 'to defend': "to drive danger or attack away", or "to take action against attack or challenge".[3] The German equivalent 'verteidigen' has a somewhat broader range of meaning, including the protection from attack as well as the attempt to repel an attack.[4]

The use of the term is not very consistent and changes depending on the circumstances. In 2006, the then German Minister of Defence Franz Josef Jung argued in favour of redefining the criteria that jus-

---

1   In the discussions about the re-establishment of a German military in 1950, opposition leader Kurt Schumacher made his party's agreement subject to the condition that any future army must be able to decide a possible war outside the German borders (Tiedtke 1986: 1).

2   Oxford Dictionary, "defence", www.lexico.com/en/definition/defence, accessed on 15-09-2019.

3   Merriam-Webster Dictionary, "defend", www.merriam-webster.com/dictionary/defend, accessed on 15-09-2019.

4   "gegen Angriffe schützen; Angriffe von jemandem, etwas abzuwehren versuchen" (Duden, "Verteidigen", www.duden.de/rechtschreibung/verteidigen#Bedeutung-1, accessed on 15-09-2019).

tify the declaration of the state of defence, recognizing the fact that such a situation might be quite different today from what the authors of the constitution had had in mind in 1949 (Löwenstein 2006: 5).

Given the changes over time and depending on one's circumstance and point of view, every person immediately has a rather specific, and likely differing, understanding of the actions, authorities, or ramifications of defence.

In international relations, the underlying connective tissue of which is the preservation of the status quo, the defending party in a conflict is usually seen as being in the favourable moral position. International relations are not, and never will be, only peaceful: aggression and even evil are traits of human behaviour and nations' actions. Thus the aggressions and evil power must be reined in. This can only be achieved through sufficient power on the part of the other actors who, at the same time, are restrained by law and moral norms (de Mazière 1993: 463). The right to self-defence is evident in conventional wisdom as well as in legal texts, and neither the Catholic Church[5] nor Martin Luther[6] have disputed the right to defend oneself.

Naturally, morality and law are not the only categories to be taken into account when discussing defence. Political and strategic considerations are just as important, and in each of these fields of study many books and papers have been written looking at different aspects of defence. The one book bringing it all together and defining and explaining the term 'defence' does not exist, and probably never

---

5   "As long as the danger of war persists and there is no international authority with the necessary competence and power, governments cannot be denied the right of lawful self-defence, once all peace efforts have failed." (Second Vatican Council (1965), Pastoral Constitution on the Church in the Modern World. Part II Chap. 5).

6   Even if a defensive action as such likely constitutes a sin, Ulrich de Maizière points out that there is no Christian life without guilt and quotes Martin Luther's "Pecca fortiter, sed crede fortius" (Sin bravely, but believe more bravely) (de Maizière 1993: 463). Hugo Grotius also presented a discussion of just war in 1625 (Grotius 1625: Book 1, 2, V–IX).

will. Too manifold are the opinions and the legitimate points of view and too rapid is the evolution in the field of international relations. Therefore, this study is by no means an attempt to provide the all-encompassing answer to the question what defence is.

Rather, this paper demonstrates and discusses a selection of relevant views on what defence could be and offers a series of conclusions for how the North Atlantic Treaty Organization (NATO) as the most important alliance for the security of the Western democracies should defend its members today.

Discussing the 'defence' of an alliance is naturally closely linked to the question of what an alliance is in today's world. A modern answer to Stephen Walt's analysis of why nations are—still—members of alliances (Walt 1987: 17–37) could shed light on the question as to what sort of defence nations expect from an alliance. This question will be touched upon, but a broad discussion of alliance theory is beyond the scope of this short paper.

This study aims to provide an overview of what the concept of defence can imply, especially when the limitations of defence become blurred, and takes a look at NATO's history with a focus on its understanding of defence. The condensed conclusions then lead to a number of observations and recommendations for NATO's future policy and its understanding of defence.

One important result is that NATO should not compete or contest, but rather retain its more defensive interpretation of defence. This includes the necessity to accept risk and even a lower level of security in exchange for a decreased risk of devastating war. In this context, parallels will be pointed out between Clausewitz's notion of ideal war and limited war on the one hand, and the idea of wars of choice and of necessity on the other, and a new concept of defence of choice and of necessity will be presented.

The other major result of the study is that NATO's best defence is its very existence: As long as NATO stands together, the Allies are safe. From this thesis two deductions can be drawn: First, cohesion must be maintained, and secondly, the Alliance as a whole must remain strong enough to ensure its security. The importance of and danger to cohesion within the Alliance will be argumentatively underlined and measures suggested for gauging the required level of strength.

Additionally, the study will show how defence has to be scalable to the threat and is likely a persistent requirement for today's NATO. Successful defence and deterrence (sic! It should not be 'deterrence and defence'!) also require flexibility in response.

To come to these conclusions, first the historical perspective will be analysed based on a choice of prominent and very different examples of concepts of defence. The chapter will also examine NATO's history from its foundation to the year 2014 with a focus on how the understanding of defence developed in the different ages of the Alliance.

The next chapter will venture into the wide field of strategy theory. First, different aspects of legal analysis will be presented, then some major strategic concepts and terms will be briefly discussed. The final section in this chapter will introduce 'Strategical Analysis', a tool to visualize and improve the understanding of strategic thinking. Strategical Analysis will then be employed to provide further insights into the nature of defence.

Chapter 4 will discuss the current phase of international relations, starting with the year 2014. This includes an analysis of the main features of the strategic environment and NATO's third age.

The final chapter will summarise the results of the previous sections and bring them together to arrive at the main conclusions. Eventually a short outlook will be presented with further remarks on some of the many questions that remain unanswered.

The strategic environment has changed immensely over the last few years and the rules-based, democracy-oriented international order is under pressure. NATO has started a process of adaptation that is far from completed. On the military level, the recent adoption of the first military strategy since 1968 signifies a major step ahead and discussions on the political side on the future of NATO continue on all levels.

It is therefore important to note that the target audience of this paper includes not only academia, but also policy makers and drafters. Some compromises on completeness and detail—but hopefully not on quality of thought!—had to be made in order to produce and publish this study in a relatively short amount of time. The COVID-19 pandemic struck in the phase of final editing, but some first observations concerning the inevitable effects of the global crisis have been included.

The paper is based solely on publicly available sources; it does not discuss the content of any classified documents or other classified information. The analysis and conclusions reflect only the private opinion of the author and do not represent an official position of NATO or the Federal Republic of Germany.

2 Defence from a Historical Perspective

When looking back on the history of war and peace, the question of right or wrong arises immediately. This chapter will not judge historical figures by asking who began a war and for what reason. There were times when war was a recognised and widely used tool to enhance a country's (or a leader's) position. It was not until the modern era, when the League of Nations was established and treaties such as the Briand-Kellogg-Pact and the Charter of the United Nations were adopted, that armed attack was banned from the toolbox of international relations. Current legal questions and their implications will be discussed in chapter 3.

Since this paper is not an attempt to rewrite Clausewitz's 'On War', this part of the paper is not supposed to be a discussion of the possible strategic, operational, or tactical superiority of offence or defence either.

For the discussion of the term 'defence', the purpose of this study, the question is rather: What was defence to different states in history? And how narrow or wide was the interpretation, what was deemed necessary to defend the state (of course, if really it was defence they sought)?

In the early 16th century, Niccolò Machiavelli conducted a related analysis of defence in his 'Discorsi'. He systematically discussed the question whether it is better to initiate or await war when a state fears to be attacked (Machiavelli 1531: 197–201). Still today these are the two extremes, but history has seen examples of a variety of nuances, some of which will be discussed below.

2.1 Nuances of Defence – Examples

2.1.1 The Great Wall of China

Even before the events Machiavelli describes had taken place, the most manifest example of a static defence was built: the Great Wall of China. Walls are, and always have been, more than infrastructure; they are also a symbol and a message, as was the Berlin Wall. Walls are not only a physical barrier; they visibly claim a defensive, protective attitude.[7] The truthfulness of this messaging depends largely on the intentions of the builder and where the wall is placed.[8]

The Great Wall of China also served and serves many purposes, mostly of a symbolic nature, i.e. of defining and separating 'us' and 'them'; only to a lesser extend does it have any defensive military value. Originally, the Great Wall served to defend settlements against nomadic tribes to the north as the Chinese were unable to defeat them and a negotiated peace was not possible either.[9] Certainly, when opportunity or necessity arose, both military expeditions and peace agreements were frequently used to increase security in the regions north of China (Bredow 2014: 38–39; Gernet et al. 1990: 42; Lovell 2006: 37). The main effort, however, was to be walls. Construction of wall segments started in the 9th century BC and was pursued for almost 3,000 years. The number of these extensions, some of which were built far into Mongolian territory, suggests that not even a wall, supposedly the embodiment of defence, is purely defensive (Lovell 2006: 43).

In the 7th century, the Great Wall was abandoned and a more aggressive approach to pacify unruly neighbours was introduced. However, under the impression of Genghis Khan's long occupation and

---

7 This was even the case with the Berlin Wall, the 'anti-fascist protection wall' ('Antifaschistischer Schutzwall') (Kubina 2011: 87). The authorities' first intention might have been to protect the people against the West, but that quickly changed to a purpose of locking in (Kubina 2011).

8 Walls in the Western Sahara and the West Bank for example have been denounced as a means of occupation of Morocco and Israel, respectively. Lovell 2006: 20–21, 349.

9 Lovell supports the view that the Wall was used as a deliberate symbol of cultural separation between the Chinese inside the Wall and the barbaric tribes beyond (Lovell 2006: 22–23, 347). Others see the Wall as merely one of many almost desperate attempts to protect Chinese territories from their aggressive northern neighbours, while still remaining open to external influences and trade (Gernet et al. 1990: 7–8).

the continuing attacks launched by his Mongolian successors, the Ming emperors reintegrated the Great Wall as the main feature of their defence and maintained it into the 17th century (Gernet et al. 1990: 46–51).

All in all, the Great Wall certainly contributed to China's security and ensured long comparatively peaceful periods. Despite its greatness though, the Wall only partly served its purposes: After its construction the enemies beyond united and forced war upon China for centuries to come (Lovell 2006: 44, 45).

The wall was employed defensively and also deep in enemy territory, and it was always accompanied by an active policy to influence the adjacent areas. So the Great Wall as a symbol suggests a more defensive attitude than it has actually served. This defensive message is one lasting effect; another one, intended or not, is a visible, deep-rooted cultural distinction between 'Chinese' and foreigners.

2.1.2 Ancient Greece: The Peloponnesian War

Thucydides' 'History of the Peloponnesian War' provides a detailed account of the struggle between Sparta and Athens in the 5th century BC. Over the centuries it has been subject of a wide variety of analyses, including Machiavelli's discussion of offence and defence (Machiavelli 1531: II–12).

What led to the outbreak of war in 460 BC and which party actually started it is—as in most cases—debatable (Bleckmann 2016: 20), but irrespective of guilt, the circumstances are interesting for the discussion in this paper.

Sparta and Athens and their respective alliances had been in a fragile balance of power before the war, resulting in a peace lasting for about 30 years.

Sparta found itself in a dilemma: Athens' power was constantly growing, raising increasing concerns in Sparta, while at the same time the Lacedaemonians felt not prepared for a long war (Murray 2013: 8). Sparta's strength was the alliance it had formed, built on trust in Sparta's loyalty and its allies' fear of Athens (Bleckmann 2016: 26–27).

Athens had spun a hegemonic network of other city-states and increasingly gained influence in the Hellenic region. To control this network and to prevail in a potential future war, Athens relied on its maritime dominance. When other poleis began to extend their maritime influence, Athens reacted and tried to expand its superiority by providing support to adversaries of those aspiring states and by underpinning its geostrategic position. To this end, Athens chose to support Corcyra against Corinth, an ally of Sparta, and to occupy Potidaea, a former Corinthian colony (Murray 2013: 7; Bleckmann 2016: 32).

These Athenian measures, intended to improve its position in the case of a future war, proved to be a self-fulfilling prophecy. After these initial offensive actions in the name of improving defence,[10] war was indeed inevitable, despite continued negotiations and communication.[11] The hegemonic rivalry as the underlying cause for conflict was complemented by 'proximate' causes stemming from the handling of a current crisis, leading to the Peloponnesian War (Koliopoulos/ Platias 1956: 28–34).

2.1.3 Ancient Rome: The Punic Wars and the Limes

Another historical series of wars between empires or alliances were the Punic Wars. With Machiavelli using them extensively as examples for the benefits of strategic offence or defence (Machiavelli 1531: II-12), they certainly merit some attention, but for a more general discussion of the nature of defence the Punic wars are only of limited use.

Conflict arose when Rome, a rising power and possible competitor (Ameling 2011: 56), disturbed the equilibrium of power between

---

10 Unlike these offensive first steps, a very passive defence served Athens well for a long time during the war. Even when faced with terrible destruction in Attica, they did not meet the Spartans in open battle, but evaded certain defeat and hoped to outlast the enemy with their superior fleet (Murray 2013: 9).

11 Thucydides (translated by Warner, Rex (1972), History of the Peloponnesian War, Hammondsworth, I-146).

Carthage and Syracuse. The theory of "defensive imperialism" claims that, after a series of wars with Carthage's involvement on Sicily, Rome was bound to intervene (Hoyos 2011: 140). According to an opposing view, Rome merely continued its expansionist policy after it had established an unthreatened hegemony over the Italian mainland. So the case can be made that the war was by no means defensive, but rather the consequential next step, even though Carthage, whose navy at the time 'could prevent the Romans even from washing their hands in the sea',[12] was not necessarily a deliberate target (Hoyos 2011: 140–141). But for the realpolitik-savvy Carthaginians a roman foothold on Sicily was a red line. So in this case war seemed to have been willingly accepted by both sides (Hoyos 2011: 141),[13] with Sicily igniting in the friction of overlapping spheres of influence, or even dominance.

When discussing defence in the context of the Roman Empire, the *limites*[14], most notably the Upper Germanic and Rhaetian Limes and the Hadrian's and Antonine Walls, come to mind. They could have been an equivalent to the Chinese Great Wall, erected as a static line of defence against barbaric tribes beyond. However, newer research suggests that the *limites* were not built for military defence (Bredow 2014: 36). In fact, they were used to channel goods and travellers through checkpoints in order to control and, if possible, tax them (Schallmayer 2006: 78). To a large extent, their original construction could have been the consequence of the Roman expeditions into

---

12 Carthage General Hanno to Roman Consul Appius Claudius in 264 BC, as reported by Diodorus (quote taken from Hoyos 2011: 140).

13 Carthaginian General Hoyos tried to avert the war when he returned captured Romans ships and crews after a first battle, but Carthage's efforts to defuse the escalation in Sicily remained half-hearted (Hoyos 2011: 145–147).

14 Singular: *limes*. The Latin term originally had a wide variety of meanings, including path, boundary line, channel, aisle or line cutting through something. It was used in many different contexts by the Romans (Moschek 2010: 7–8; Schallmayer 2006: 11).

those areas, as their military doctrine included the use of *limites* to sustain attacks and protect flanks (Moschek 2010: 19–25; Schallmayer 2006: 11–13). The later employment of the limites as demarcations of the boundaries of the Roman Empire ("limites imperii et ripae"[15]) is nevertheless remarkable. It represents the shift from the expansionist Rome of Cicero ("The borders of the [Roman] provinces extend as far as [our] spears and swords reach!"[16]) that lasted until the reign of Emperor Trajan to the acceptance of an outer limit under Emperor Hadrian and a more or less fixed definition of the Roman Empire (Schallmayer 2006: 16–17). The 'manifest destiny' of ancient Europe had reached its final frontier. By specifying to where the Roman Empire extended—and with it not only foreign rule and taxes, but also Roman law and a certain degree of culture and modernity—the area was defined that was to be defended by Rome through tactics that varied from region to region and century to century.[17] So the focus shifted from actors that had to be defeated or checked to an area that was to be controlled. For many groups and individuals who sought trade or security within the borders of the Roman Empire, the limites also were a line of aspiration marking the threshold to the 'developed world'. This is the reason why the limites were also used to control border crossings and channel the flow of goods and people (Schallmayer 2006: 76–79).

---

15   Latin: "Borders of the empire and rivers" (Schallmayer 2006: 14).
16   "fines provinciae fuerint qui gladiorum atque pilorum" (Schallmayer 2006: 16).
17   A detailed discussion of the different approaches with a view to defence would be certainly valuable, but by far exceeds the scope of this paper. For a comprehensive analysis of how the Roman strategy shifted from a buffer zone of vassal states to the defence of a defined boundary to a defence-in-depth approach, see Luttwak 2016.

2.1.4 The Truman Doctrine and Containment

A modern day example for a confrontational defensive[18] policy is the US containment policy laid down in the Truman Doctrine. It followed George Kennan's call to confront Soviet activities with superior counterforce wherever the security interests of the West were threatened (Crabb 1982: 131–132).[19] President Truman's predecessor, Franklin Roosevelt, had already foreseen a threat emanating from Soviet expansionism, and Truman, a stern anti-communist, formulated his doctrine in a speech to Congress in 1947. It was implemented by a multitude of measures to confront Soviet activities without geographic limitation, and with a variety of means reaching from financial aid to covert or open military force (Crabb 1982: 117–118, 121–124). Facing the threat of communism and potential Marxist revolutions, the spread of prosperity, if necessary through US aid, was a central function of containment (Grillo 2003: 52–53).

Containment tried to find middle ground between the extreme American positions of aggression and preventive war on one side, and a return to isolationism on the other (Crabb 1982: 150–152). It is widely recognised as one of the most influential American presidential doctrines (Crabb 1982: 108).

The defensive necessity of the containment policy was heavily discussed at the time of its implementation as well as by historians with the hindsight of its successes and limitations. Truman's intentions were certainly driven by the concrete fear that vital US interests, such as access to the energy reserves in the Gulf Region, could only be defended by containing Soviet expansion (Grillo 2003: 49). But he also had idealistic and ideological motives, seeing the US as the nation "the free peoples of the world [...] look to for support in maintaining their freedom" (Truman 1947), and returning to the view that for

---

18 For a detailed review of the academic discussion as to whether containment was indeed defensive see: Trombley Averill 2012: 411–413.

19 Kennan later claimed he had only intended to promote a political containment of communism (Crabb 1982: 149–50).

the US peace was indivisible, and aggression anywhere endangered its security (Hunt 1987: 155–161).[20]

While not judging the policy as right or wrong, the described combination of Truman's motives makes it likely that while objectively opposition to Soviet actions was necessary, the purely defensive requirements could have been fulfilled with a less confrontational approach. The strategic and economic superiority of the United States gave the presidents some leeway as to where to draw the line of confrontation without facing immediate disastrous consequences[21]. This is also indicated by the fact that neither President Eisenhower's and John Foster Dulles' 'roll-back'-approach nor the phase of less hawkish policies under President Carter led to immediate loss or victory in the Cold War.

President Reagan chose a more competitive policy again; he was not content with mere containment and called for actively pushing back communism, a policy that resulted in American military and economic assistance to anti-communist insurgencies throughout the world (Warner 2003: 98–99, 116–117). This approach can hardly be called defensive anymore, so to what extent Reagan's policy contributed to the end of the Cold War is left for other studies to discuss.

2.1.5 The Arab-Israeli Six-Day War

The Six-Day War offers an example of a preventive strike to serve a nation's defence. Going further than Machiavelli in his Discorsi, the example could even build a case not only for the possible advantage of a preventive strike, but even for its necessity in cases where the very survival of a state is at stake. Advocating a mobile and flexible form of warfighting, Hans von Seeckt in 1930 explicitly included a

---

20 Hunt describes the language used for communists in US secret national security papers and approved by Truman with 'stark and sweeping terms usually reserved for crusades' (Hunt 1987: 158).
21 Although it could be argued that with a less confrontational approach the US might have been spared the bitter experience of the Vietnam War.

pre-emptive strike in his understanding of national defence—enabled through modern warfighting.[22]

Carl von Clausewitz of course considered the defence to be structurally superior to the offence, but Johann Schmid tries to use the Six-Day War to prove Clausewitz wrong (Schmid 2006: 608–610).[23] His conclusion is based on the assumption that the Israeli airstrike on 5 June 1967 constituted the beginning of a strategic attack performed by an inferior army.

However, one could also argue that the air attack was only a tactical-operational strike, involving surprise, the genius of the field marshal, the fog of war and other concepts developed by Clausewitz. Due to the overwhelming success, the Israeli forces had obtained air supremacy and could then commence the offensive campaign from a position of strength.

Regardless of the outcome of this discussion, the case can be built that the situation of a particular nation could require preventive offensive action to secure its very existence. The necessity for a geographically small state to ensure its very survival by force was one of

---

22 "Der Gedanke moderner Kriegsführung bleibt damit durchaus auf den Begriff der Landesverteidigung gegründet, gleichviel ob ein Land einer Bedrohung zuvorzukommen sich gezwungen sieht oder ob es einen schon eingeleiteten Angriff des Feindes abwehrt. Im ersten Fall bietet nur der schnell und kräftig ausgeführte Schlag Aussicht, den drohenden Absichten zuvorzukommen und sie zu vereiteln; im zweiten ist der Staat im Nachteil, vielleicht schon verloren, der dem Einbruch eines starken und zugleich beweglichen Heeres zur Abwehr erst die langsam arbeitende Maschinerie des Volksheeres entgegenzusetzen hat." (Seeckt 1930: 69–70).

23 In trying to prove Clausewitz wrong, Schmid refers to yet another example illustrating the superiority of the operational action 'attack', namely the 12th battle of the Isonzo in 1917 (Schmid 2011: 137–151). Here the German and Austro-Hungarian troops attacked from—and because of—a position of weakness, but defeated the superior Italian army. However, the battle is an example from the operational level and therefore not suitable for this analysis.

the arguments causing the international community to not generally condemn the Israeli offensive. Another line of thought saw the Egyptian blocking of the port of Eilat as use of force and the Israeli actions therefore as legitimate defence (Shaw 2017: 866).

2.2 Defence in NATO History

Naturally, there is an abundance of books and articles on NATO's history, and this study is explicitly not meant to be just another one. Most works focus on the description of the phases of the organisation's history, the turning points, its inner dynamics or setup, its many different roles or on the transatlantic partnership or NATO's relationship to the European Union.[24] Certainly within many of these analyses NATO's interpretation of defence is touched upon, however, for this study it was deemed necessary to walk through NATO's history with a particular focus on its understanding of defence. How did NATO defend or intend to defend the Alliance in the different phases? And how does this affect the Allies' sense of self and NATO's role in today's world?

The setup of this paper does not allow for a comprehensive discussion of the whole of NATO's lively history, but the brief analysis will follow the lines of 'the three ages of NATO', an expression used by Secretary General Jens Stoltenberg (Stoltenberg 2016). The first age covers the bipolar confrontation with the USSR, the second age spans the period marked by out-of-area operations after the end of the Cold War until 2014 when NATO entered its third age, a phase characterised by a complex strategic environment with both more assertive state actors employing conventional and hybrid means as well as threats posed by international terrorists.

This historical section of the paper will consequently first look at the foundation of NATO and the Treaty itself and what the inten-

---

24 For a brief, yet comprehensive and recent discussion see for example Sloan 2016: 10–18.

tions for defence were at the time. Then the first and the second ages of NATO will be described. The third, contemporary age will be discussed in chapter 4 'Defence today'.

2.2.1 Foundation of NATO

As described above, in 1947 US President Truman explained to the US Congress what he deemed necessary to defend the Western world from the threat of Soviet expansionism, without naming communism explicitly (Truman 1947). This was the beginning of the Truman Doctrine and containment, ending American isolationism and leading to the US entering the competition for the free world with the USSR. Notably, this policy was defined before NATO came into existence and before the US could legally join defence treaties in peacetime.[25]

In 1948 the western European countries Great Britain, France, Belgium, the Netherlands and Luxembourg included a mutual defence clause in their Brussels Treaty, declaring: "should [a party to the treaty] be the object of an armed attack in Europe, the other High Contracting Parties will, in accordance with the provisions of Article 51 of the Charter of the United Nations, afford the Party so attacked all the military and other aid and assistance in their power." (Brussels Treaty 1948: Art IV). They also included provisions to promote development and cooperation, but did not intend to extend their efforts beyond the parties to the treaty (Brussels Treaty 1948: Art. I, II, VII). Under the increasing threat of communism the parties to the treaty agreed to a very far-reaching provision for collective defence. Clearly their focus was to assure each other of their respective support, but there was no intention similar to the US containment policy.

These two approaches in the face of a common threat were brought together in the foundation of the North Atlantic Treaty Organization in 1949. The intention to form a collective security agreement for the

---

25 This was authorized only after the US constitution was changed, following the so-called Vandenberg Resolution 239 of the US-Senate on 11 June 1948 (Stupka 2008: 140–141).

North Atlantic was first publicly announced by President Truman in his inaugural address after his re-election in 1949 (Anslover 2014: 118–119). The Europeans secured the guarantees of an overwhelming economic power with advanced conventional capabilities and a nuclear arsenal for their protection and gained the strategic depth to possibly outlast a Soviet attack. For the US, NATO was one of several measures to implement the principle of containment (Crabb 1982: 139–140). Truman himself claimed that NATO was another expression of the principles of the Truman Doctrine (Trombley Averill 2012: 421).

Containment thinking was reflected in the composition of the founding Allies, going beyond the group of nations of the Brussels Treaty. Italy for example was included as a founding member despite concerns regarding its military value and reliability only to keep it from turning to communism and subsequently allowing the USSR's influence to spread in the Mediterranean region (Trombley Averill 2012: 421). However, already the first round of NATO enlargement did no longer follow that rationale, showing the emancipation of NATO from the containment thought.

In the North Atlantic Treaty itself, NATO Allies define two aims of the organisation: First [sic] to accept and further the goals of the Charter of the United Nations, and secondly to protect their freedom and further stability and well-being in the treaty area. Both aims are absolute, they are neither established in comparison to others nor directed against a specific actor and they apply under all circumstances. This already defines NATO's role beyond that of a purely military alliance for collective defence. It has been widely accepted that activities are not limited to the Allies' territory or the defined treaty area (Varwick/Woyke 2000: 149–150), but nevertheless all provisions clearly show the defensive and reactive setup of the organisation.[26]

Compared with the Brussels Treaty, the central collective defence Article 5 is formulated rather softly:

---

26   For a detailed discussion of the North Atlantic Treaty see Varwick/Woyke 2000: 24–31, or Stupka 2007: 145–171.

The Parties agree that an armed attack against one or more of them in Europe or North America shall be considered an attack against them all and consequently they agree that, if such an armed attack occurs, each of them, in exercise of the right of individual or collective self-defence recognised by Article 51 of the Charter of the United Nations, will assist the Party or Parties so attacked by taking forthwith, individually and in concert with the other Parties, such action as it deems necessary, including the use of armed force, to restore and maintain the security of the North Atlantic area. [...]" (North Atlantic Treaty Organization 1949: Article 5)

The Allies are only obliged to provide support 'as deemed necessary' leaving the national governments some room for manoeuvre and thus alleviating American fears of too far-reaching entanglement. Also the purpose of the organisation going beyond the pure provision of security stemmed from a mixture of appeal to American idealism in order to secure domestic support in the US, American economic interest to shape an open and stable Western community beyond military cooperation and true idealism of the founding fathers.[27]

2.2.2 First Age of NATO

The first age of NATO began with its foundation and spans the period of the two-bloc confrontation of the Cold War. Key to NATO's survival in its first age and the ability to influence the course of history and to 'stand up to the bullies of the international arena' was the firm unity of the Allies and the commitment to collective defence. That way NATO successfully protected the Allies, its territory and its people (Stoltenberg 2016).

In the early phase of the Alliance, NATO had the luxury of a nuclear monopoly and the fact that the US mainland could not be threatened

---

27   Trombley Averill suggests the term 'practical idealism' for this combination of intentions (Trombley Averill 2012: 415–420).

directly. Nevertheless, the original intention was to build up a NATO force that could conventionally defend Europe against a potential Soviet invasion, even though that aspiration quickly proved unrealistic (Thoß 2006: 3, 5). Even with West Germany as a member of the Alliance, the USSR retained a strong conventional superiority.

As a result the nuclear component was considered to be primarily a deterrent, but it was also an integral part of the defence strategy as a compromise between threat and feasible defence (Thoß 2006: 39–42). While conventional forces were to delay enemy forces as far eastwards of the river Rhine as possible, strategic nuclear airstrikes were to defeat the attack and prepare the counterattack to reclaim lost territory (MC 14/1 1952: 9., 10.; Militärgeschichtliches Forschungsamt 1975: 48). So at that time, NATO had a very clear idea of military defence, including explicitly offensive components,[28] and how it was to be conducted.

Not quite so clearly defined were required actions short of military defence. The defence policy of NATO in peacetime was "to convince the USSR that war does not pay, and to insure a successful defense of the NATO Area should war occur." (MC 14/1 1952: 2). Plans to achieve this were to follow certain principles, including "to oppose, by all measures short of war, any peacetime attempts by the USSR or her satellites to increase their threat against the Treaty nations; meanwhile, initiating measures to exploit Soviet weaknesses." (MC 14/1 1952: 2.a). Clearly this implied a wide range of activities in peacetime, but what this could comprise was left to unspecified subordinate plans, the execution of which remains unclear. Also the scope was limited: the actions were to oppose attempts to increase the threat against the Allies, which means they were not aimed at the Soviets per se. Similarly, the last part of the paragraph at first glance suggests a hint of competitiveness, but again it is heavily caveated. Subsequent plans were not to exploit Soviet weaknesses; they were

---

28 "The general plan for the employment of NATO air forces must be offensive from the outset." (MC 14/1 1952: 15).

only to initiate measures to exploit them, with the execution of the exploitation supposedly following in times of war. Throughout the strategic document MC 14/1, any offensive action of NATO against the Soviet states is clearly limited to times of war, including the Overall Strategic Aim, beginning with "Should they [the Allies] be drawn into war, [...]" (MC 14/1 1952: 9). Only then NATO would have had to defend and follow through with the plan to "destroy the will and capability of the USSR and her satellites to wage war" (MC 14/1 1952: 9), as Clausewitz would have put it.

MC 14/3 eventually was a codification of an understanding of NATO strategy that had taken shape, in conceptual and factual terms, over the decade leading to its adoption (Wittmann 2001: 220).

In the strategic language used by NATO during the Cold War and the 'Flexible Response'[29] phase, the term 'direct defence' expressed the most conservative understanding of defence. It described the denial of an attacker's war aims on the same level of escalation that the enemy has chosen (Magenheimer 1986: 20). It meant conventional defence against a conventional attack, but also included—after NATO had introduced tactical nuclear weapons—the employment of non-conventional means if the Warsaw Pact had chosen that level of escalation. The use of the term "forward defence" in this respect referred to a conventional defence close to the border to the attacker. It did not exclude strikes or counterattacks on the aggressor's territory, but was not intended to be pre-emptive or offensive (Magenheimer 1986: 70–73).

The next doctrinal step was 'deliberate escalation'. This included the employment of nuclear weapons in order to clearly demonstrate to the attacker that NATO is willing to use their nuclear arsenal and that the continuation of aggression cannot be profitable. It could also include strikes to decisively weaken the attacker or exploit its

---

29 Introduced with North Atlantic Treaty Organization, Military Commitee (1968), MC 14/3. Overall Strategic Concept for the Defense of the North Atlantic Treaty Organization Area, Brussels.

weaknesses (Magenheimer 1986: 20–21). While the first purpose leans more towards a pure deterrence intention, the latter makes 'pre-planned escalation' part of Alliance defence strategy.

The third stage, the 'general nuclear response' meant the employment of strategic nuclear weapons, mostly against an opponent's strategic nuclear capabilities (Magenheimer 1986: 20–21). In times of mutual assured destruction (MAD) of the opposing parties, this level of escalation cannot be regarded as part of defence as it is unlikely to end or limit the impact on one's own nation or population.

In the 1980s, scholars suggested that NATO should have offensive options at its disposal and claimed that a purely defensive mind-set—a "Maginot-line mentality without the Maginot line" (The Economist 1981: 15)—would not be sufficient.

Samuel Huntington argued in 1984 that NATO as a defensive alliance does not necessarily require a defensive strategy: "NATO is a defensive alliance politically, which means that its purpose is to protect its members against Soviet attack through deterrence if possible and defense if necessary. There is, however, no reason why a politically defensive alliance cannot have a militarily offensive strategy. Such a strategy may, indeed, be essential to securing the deterrent purposes of the alliance." (Huntington 1984: 45). He then goes on arguing for conventional (operational level) offensives as part of NATO doctrine. Simplistically, this approach could be labelled 'counterattacking', and where and when counterattacks would have been employed, hopefully would have been a decision made by the military leadership of the Alliance. However, Huntington's thinking in military categories and terms such as 'initiative' was intended to compel the Warsaw Pact into a different posture even in peacetime, or—in modern US doctrinal terms—in competition short of armed conflict.[30]

Neither the North Atlantic Council nor individual Allies have ever embraced such an offensive approach to defence. Apart from ques-

---

30   See section 3.2.5 (Contest).

tions of feasibility,[31] this might have been a consequence of the proponents' failure to sufficiently explain how Warsaw Pact decision makers should differentiate between preparations for such retaliatory offensives and proper attacks. At the very least, any such political contemplations or visible preparations as laid out by Huntington (Huntington 1984: 53) and others (Gates 1991: 53) would have been a heyday for Soviet propaganda writers. This points directly to the security dilemma and the side effects a competitive strategy can generate.

In 1968, with the newly adopted MC 14/3 and just after the Soviet intervention in Czechoslovakia, the narrow interpretation of 'defensive' within NATO became visible and was officially underlined. In reaction to the Soviet aggression the importance of both the nuclear and conventional deterrent, the deployment of troops inside NATO territory and increased budgets were discussed. With a view to bolstering the defence of Europe, German Defence Minister Schröder addressed three issues, all of them looking to the inside of the Alliance: strengthening the transatlantic bond, improving co-operation in procedures and armament in Europe, and alignment of nuclear and conventional armament (Schröder 1968: 7, 13–14).

Clearly, with Flexible Response, Allies hat to widen their spectrum in development and tactics. A conventional war or a conventional portion of a war beyond the first phase of delay was thinkable again, and new forces and structures needed to be built. In the early 1970s the Warsaw Pact had about twice as many fixed-wing aircraft stationed in middle Europe than the NATO members (Interavia 1972: 963). To compensate for the gap Allies concentrated on development in quality and numbers, but conventional parity was never achieved.

Nevertheless, the defensive approach never grew more confrontational. Denmark and more significantly Norway entered the Alliance only with caveats in order to minimise provocation of or proximity to

---

31   For a critique of retaliatory offensives from a military strategic point of view see: Gates 1991: 53–57.

Soviet forces. They favoured a 'Nordic Balance', together with neutral Sweden and Finland, over maximizing a strategic advantage (Engelmann 1978: 138–139), even in the face of Soviet activities against Norway and in the Baltic Sea in the late 1970s.[32]

Even in the relatively clear-cut confrontation of the Cold War, discussions about NATO's strategy and how to implement it were fierce. Back then, there was no blueprint for a perfect strategy and the Allies' security interests were already too diverse to easily find a common political denominator (Tiedtke 1986: 5); and now, with an increasingly complex security environment, the arithmetic has gotten even more difficult.

The interpretation of defence had always been a contentious issue, mostly with the US pushing for more proactivity and the European Allies concentrating on Alliance territory and non-confrontational policies. For example, when US President Carter pushed again for an increased involvement of NATO in reaction to the Soviet invasion in Afghanistan, the Alliance refused and suggested agreements of individual governments with the US to provide assistance. The European partners interpreted the Soviet move as less aggressive and were afraid of a confrontational approach and the possible diversion of NATO strength. Only Turkey supported the US policy and urged NATO Allies to join (Crabb 1982: 354–355, 359).

One could assume that even if NATO's defence policy was not competitive, at least its membership policy was. Particularly, one might be inclined to suspect NATO of having pursued the admission of Turkey with its extraordinary geostrategic importance to improve the Alliance's strategic position vis-á-vis the USSR. However, the opposite was the case. It was Turkey that had begun pushing for membership since the foundation of NATO and increased its efforts in 1950, with

---

32 These activities included air-/sea-space infractions, reckless manoeuvres, and attempts to obstruct exercises (Engelmann 1978: 144–145). The latest Russian attempts of harassing NATO assets and testing reactions to infringements follow a similar pattern.

NATO being reluctant and first offering only a partnership status (McGhee 1990: 72–75). It was only after Turkey's strong engagement in the Korean War[33] that the US changed its policy and supported the membership. Great Britain also supported the admission (having bilateral treaty obligations anyway (McGhee 1990: 74) and France offered support in exchange for a naval command position in the NATO force structure, but still the other Allies only reluctantly agreed, partly against their own judgement. Particularly the northern Europeans shared a view that the NATO purpose of defending the North Atlantic Area should not be diluted (McGhee 1990: 87–88)—a thought that was also expressed by the US Joint Chiefs of Staff, clearly indicating that despite Turkey's considerable military strength and geographic importance, its admission into NATO was rather considered a burden than an advantage (McGhee 1990: 72).

2.2.3 Second Age of NATO

The second age of NATO began with the fall of the Berlin Wall and the dissolution of the Warsaw Pact and the USSR in the early 1990s. Many predictions made after the end of the Cold War quickly proved wrong, but some fundamental and irreversible changes did take place.[34] The fall of the Iron Curtain was not the end of history (Fukuyama 1992), but rather the beginning of a new chapter. In its second age, NATO reacted to new challenges and moved from pure collective defence to managing conflicts beyond its borders (Stoltenberg 2016).

How did this influence the Alliance's view on defence?

---

33 Turkey was the second nation after the US to pledge troops to the UN intervention and provided an army brigade that showed exceptional valour in battle as part of the 2nd US Division. About two thirds of the Turkish troops were killed or wounded in action, saving a great number of American soldiers. (McGhee 1990: 77–78).

34 These changes include the collapse of the expansionist Communist movement; the end of Soviet dominance over Central and Eastern Europe; the democratic revolutions in these countries; Germany's reunification; and the dissolution of the Warsaw Pact (Wittmann 2001: 220).

One expectation was that the first line of NATO's defence would be found outside of its territory (Comité Strategique 1996: 26). This had always been a demand particularly of the former front-states and now, without a direct military threat to NATO and with a changed nature of conflict, it finally seemed achievable and also necessary. The military requirements of this 'new defence' were intelligence assets, mobility and a forward deployment of troops for situational awareness, reaction to crises and preparation for possible reinforcements. Defence in the 'old' sense, mostly air- and sea-policing and measures of emergency preparation and resilience, was superseded in importance by the more civilian tasks of 'protection' and 'security' (Comité Strategique 1996: 29–33). With the more comprehensive notion of security as the strategic basis of NATO on the one hand (Wittmann 2001: 224) and then the first invocation of Article 5 after the attacks of 9/11 on the other, the Alliance returned to its full raison d'ètre as laid down in the Treaty. Yet, particularly the fast, univocal and unrestricted solidarity to the US after the attacks of 9/11, the unforeseen and to a large extent unintended level of commitment in Afghanistan[35] and the subsequent fight against terrorism challenged some Allies that were not yet fully prepared for military engagements of that magnitude (Hacke 2004: 33–34).

The responsibility for the Alliance's strategic orientation moved from the Military Committee to the Council, and the Strategic Concepts and military implementation documents in the MC 400 to MC 400/3 series replaced the military strategies of the MC 14/1 to 14/3. The Strategic Concepts outlined a strategy without an adversary focussing on stability as a positive objective, and defence was not the focal point of the military. The former linear defence in Central Europe was given up and in the new spectrum of peace, crisis and war, the military was to keep a protected peace, rather than provide the defence of the Alliance. Still some principles stayed alive, such as the intention to keep aggressors out of the Allies' territory or defeat pos-

---

35   See section 3.2.3 (The Security Dilemma) of this paper.

sible attacks as early as possible—an approach formerly known as "forward defence". If anything, the flexibility of forces and responses needed to increase, even with the term 'flexible response' being too closely linked to Cold War thinking and abandoned with the Strategic Concepts (Wittmann 2001: 222–224).

The first Strategic Concept of 1991 still mentioned the aim of preserving the strategic balance within Europe, but that was no longer seen appropriate in the 1999 revision. The revision of the Strategic Concept in 1999 kept the core principles of NATO unchanged and to a large part aimed at preventing Allies from returning to national security policies (Wittmann 2001: 222, 227–230).

This only partly succeeded; particularly the US policy of unilateral action under the George W. Bush administration led to a decreased importance of NATO (Hacke 2004: 32). With its intervention in the Kosovo conflict in 1999, NATO demonstrated the willingness and an ability to operate preventively. Certainly humanitarian aspects and the intention to influence the political development of the Balkan region played a crucial role in the decision-making, but the forceful projection of stability in Europe also increased the security of the Allies. Thus the intervention served a defensive purpose.[36] Yet, the interpretation that it was conflict prevention that resulted in the US-led engagement in Iraq in 2003 went too far for a large portion of the Allies, straining the cohesion of the Alliance and hindering its ability to act and adapt. Adding to the frustration on either side, the operations in Afghanistan and Iraq displayed a considerable capability gap between the US and the European Allies. This triggered a vicious circle, the effects of which still affect NATO policy: European governments and societies felt they could only provide second class effects and were—conveniently—limited to clean up after the US had finished the fighting. This led to a lack of responsibility and public interest, which again led to insufficient engagement, funding and capability

---

36   A good overview of the different aspects is provided by Stupka 2008: 219–223.

development, further increasing the capability gap. In many cases, societies and politicians were not fully cognisant of the changes in the security landscape and what these changes meant for the employment of the military. German Minister of Defence Jung acknowledged in 2006 "the international commitments already entered by Germany have neither been fully registered by the population, nor by the majority of the members of parliament." (Löwenstein 2006: 5).

In addition to the differing security interests, NATO in its second phase had to deal with different threats to security,[37] making it already unlikely that a one-size-fits-all approach to defence could be applied to all sources of global conflict (Wirtz 2005: 383, 386). Even today the definition of what constitutes terrorism remains difficult and differs between nations (Shaw 2017: 884).

Nevertheless, the newly emerged risks and the necessary wider approach to security and possibly defence were discussed and respective policies were adopted. The tasks of 'Collective Defence', 'Crisis Management', and 'Cooperative Security' on the one hand and 'Deterrence and Defence', 'Projecting Stability', and 'Fight against Terrorism' on the other overlap each other. So conceptually, even 'Projecting Stability' and 'Fight against Terrorism' should actively contribute to the Collective Defence of NATO.

After the end of the Cold War, NATO considerably enlarged its membership to include former members of the Warsaw Pact. A school of academic thought saw the political task of stabilising these young democracies in Eastern Europe as the central task of NATO in its second age.[38] Clearly these enlargements were not intended to improve NATO's strategic position against a potential adversary, but they were based on the free will of the nations to join an attractive Alliance to provide for their enduring security and further their European integration.

---

37 In NATO documents the term 'risk' was now preferred over 'threats' (Wittmann 2001: 220).

38 Haglund 2002: 37–45, quoted in: Luhde/Tiede 2003: 2.

In NATO's second age the western countries were confronted with a broad range of threats against which deterrence proved ineffective: "some actors—al Quaeda is a case in point—simply are not deterred by America's overwhelming military capability and its clearly demonstrated willingness to go to the ends of the earth to retaliate in the wake of undesirable action" (Wirtz 2005: 384). This vastly changed the balance of deterrence and defence and the perception of how security is provided. Wirtz described this change in 2005 as follows:

> Deterrence succeeds not by fighting wars [...] but by preventing them from occurring. During the Cold War, this statement appeared obvious, but today, young "warfighters" find the notion that fighting is synonymous with failure in a deterrence relationship to be counterintuitive, or at least contradictory to their military experience (Wirtz 2005: 388).

In the second age of NATO, military interventions and operations in the fight against terrorism became part of defence. Not the absence of war, but victory in battle became the indicator for successful defence and security.

The second age also brought some changes that were not directly security-related, but nevertheless changed the face of international relations. Even before the shift to the third age in 2014, the financial crisis beginning in 2008 and the rise of former regional or emerging powers hinted at a change in the political landscape, including increasing limitations to the US hegemony. Budgetary and economic considerations became part of security politics (Keller 2012: 1, 3).

After the demise of international terrorism following the intervention in Afghanistan the most imminent threat to the security of the Western nations did not stem from an actor in the international system, rather, it was the threats to the system itself (Keller 2012: 2, 4).

Additionally, the US administration saw the future of the century being decided in the Pacific region and intended to 'pivot' that way and shape and 'update' existing partnerships and alliances for that future (Clinton 2011). This could have involved a stronger role for

NATO in Europe (and maybe the UN), but that failed to materialize. The European Allies suffered the same problems as the US, and their security and assertiveness depended to a large extend on the perceived US ability and willingness to act (Keller 2012: 3).

2.3 Thoughts on Defence in History

In his Discorsi, Machiavelli came to the conclusion that for some states it is advantageous to lead a war offensively while others should remain defensive. For him keeping the war away was generally desirable for states with an unarmed population and disadvantageous geography. If a state's people were well equipped and fit for warfighting, however, the attack should be waited for in order to be able to fight in one's own territory (Machiavelli 1531: 201).

Transferring this thinking to today's world is hardly possible. The effects of the next big war would affect populations regardless of their proximity to battle, and an armed populous is hardly as much a decisive factor in technologically advanced times as it used to be in Florence in the 16th century. Russia has in the past benefitted more than once from its stress-resistant population and vast distances, so indeed for the Russian Federation the defensive approach has proven its value. However, NATO Allies' highly developed and infrastructure-dependent societies today are neither suited to endure a war that was brought to them, nor are they suited to endure and accept a war that first struck the adversary. So for NATO the most imminent question is not where or how to best fight a defensive war, but how to prevent it.

This paper cannot offer a thorough analysis of the whole history of war and peace or even of the examples briefly introduced. However, some relevant thoughts can be carved out.

As explained in previous sections, even measures proclaimed as defensive—such as walls regularly are, or collective defence alliances—can have offensive aspects to them. The decisive factor is not so much the label or the rhetoric, but rather the underlying intention and pursued policy.

At the same time, rhetoric does matter. Communicating through strong language or symbols can engrave division lines and cement conflict over extended periods of time.

Athens deemed it necessary to have the best possible position secured should war with Sparta break out. A consequence of that aspired superiority was that war indeed broke out – Athens eventually lost and with it its hegemonic position, in spite of its early preparations. Perceived strategic necessities need to be carefully balanced with their immediate deteriorating influence on the strategic environment.

The Punic Wars were not an example of defensive behaviour, but rather of spheres of influence or dominance colliding. But even defensive entities not thinking in these categories have to keep in mind that their aspirations or desired end-states—supposing a strategy can actually have an end-state (a point that will be discussed later in this paper)—could be incompatible with those of other actors. Moderation in aims to strive for could replace many perceived defensive necessities.

The fact that Rome's *limites* were used to control migration and trade rather than for military defence shows that Rome in many areas was able to persuade by soft power and that the Empire was attractive as a provider of stability and development. Also the *limites* marked a shift from defeating antagonistic actors to defending a geographic area. These could be valuable hints from a distant past for an Alliance with no specific adversary named in its Treaty and set up to protect its members and foster a rules-based international order.

The Truman Doctrine was formulated before NATO was conceived. The Alliance can be interpreted as the military defensive part of the containment policy for the North Atlantic and Europe, notwithstanding the fact that containment comprised more than just the vitally essential elements for defence.

In the Six-Day War, Israel had good military and legal arguments for its pre-emptive air strikes. Securing the very existence of a state is a powerful argument, however, it is hardly applicable to any NATO Ally. The very purpose of membership is and always has been the guarantee of the Allies' security. Not every aspect of the nations' integrity—or even territorial sovereignty—can always be guaranteed, as is demonstrated by the early defence planning concerning the frontline states, today's cyber and disinformation attacks, and any model of a potential Russian attack on the Baltic states, but the heart of NATO is the trust that in any case the full integrity of all Allies will be restored. For this NATO has always relied on its strategic depth, knowing that its geography and the political nature of the Alliance, including its slow decision-making processes, inhibit flexible or surprising action and were a disadvantage even of a forward defence (Roth 1989: 35, 39–40).[39] Additionally, NATO comprises members who are traditionally not fond of strong talk of pre-emptive or preventive war and who champion cooperation, diplomacy, and disarmament as preferred strategies, at least in their neighbourhoods (Wirtz 2005: 384).

In the founding process of NATO the close proximity to containment was visible, but the Alliance quickly emancipated itself and developed its own policy that was explicitly not competitive, neither in actions nor in membership policy. The comparatively weak Article 5, obliging Allies only to the collective defence efforts deemed necessary, favours non-entanglement over guaranteed support in the spectrum covered by the alliance dilemma. This requires all members, but particularly the US, to focus on displayed cohesion from the outset to assure exposed Allies and deter potential adversaries.

In the first age of NATO the possible employment of nuclear weapons as part of defence blurred the line between deterrence and defence. The distinction remains difficult to the day and will be discussed later in this paper.

---

39 In this respect NATO exemplifies quite the opposite of Friedrich II., who favoured a largely offensive strategy striving for quick decisive victories partly because of Prussia's inability to sustain a longer war (Schmid 2011: 40–41).

An offensive component of defence was deliberately not considered and also the organisation's membership policy and the policies of its new members concentrated on a non-competitive posture.

After the end of the Cold War NATO had to react and adapt. Following Machiavelli and recognizing the nature of NATO's societies, the possibility to carry the fight against adversaries into their territory was an opportunity. But new questions arose; the famous statement that NATO must go 'out-of-area or out of business' summarizes the challenge very pointedly. When phrasing this, US Senator Lugar had a scenario in mind reminding him of the time after World War I. He saw out-of-area operations a necessary for the defence of the Alliance.[40] However, with the exception of the Article 5 response to 9/11, NATO operations in its second age were never defensive in a legal sense.[41] It remains to be discussed whether the Allies' attempts to increase their security by pushing away instability geographically and in terms of probability can or should be considered as 'defence' in NATO strategic language.

In any case, the new tasks led to a transformation of capabilities towards more mobility, flexibility and capabilities able to shape the environment beyond NATO's territory. Also within NATO territory complexity has increased with new aspects of defence arising and many fields of defence becoming intermingled with questions of resilience and the responsibilities of other authorities tasked with providing security.

The on-going operations in the name of increased security for the Alliance have also changed what is perceived as 'producing security'. In the first age of NATO the belittled waiting for the Soviet attack, the absence of war and battle used to be the expression of security. In the second age victory in battle and successful drone strikes became visible images of security. This has important ramifications for the third age of NATO.

---

40 Richard Lugar, quoted in: Rosenfeld 1993.
41 This point will be addressed below in section 3.1.1 (Public International Law).

3 Theories of and Approaches to Defence

The second chapter has provided some insight into and inspiration from how leaders have acted in different situations in history. Just as international law emerges out of state practice, the vocabulary and thinking of strategy is influenced by the empirical analysis of what was said and done in critical turning points of history.

Another source for strategic thinking is the analytical work published by academics, or military or political practitioners of strategy. There are countless fields of expertise and points of view that are relevant to the analysis of strategy and, more specifically, of defence. Within those fields of expertise such as philosophy, political science, law, military science, or psychology, just to name a few, again countless schools of thought or predispositions make for endless variations of conclusions. Consequently any overview of analytical thinking on strategy is bound to be incomplete, but the attempt has to be made to touch upon the most important features.

This chapter comprises one section on some legal aspects of defence, and a second section will briefly discuss some strategic concepts and theories, mostly from a political science perspective, as they pertain to the questions of defence targeted in this paper. In the third section a model to visualize and define strategic thinking will be introduced and employed to clarify notions of defence.

The third source of strategic thinking would be the genius or the creativity of the decision maker or drafter of a strategy. This process is not covered directly in this paper, but if a strategist's ideas were implemented or published at some point, his or her ideas have become historical or academic sources, respectively.

3.1 Judicial Views on Defence

Defence and self-defence are not only important concepts in international law; they also serve to differentiate between criminal and legitimate actions in criminal law, providing some background for the understanding of what defence is.

The pertinent provision in British law is: "It is both good law and good sense that a man who is attacked may defend himself. It is both good law and good sense that he may do, but only do, what is reasonably necessary."[42] One of the important US rulings in this respect was: "When a person has reasonable grounds for believing, and does in fact actually believe, that danger of his being killed, or of receiving great bodily harm, is imminent, he may act on such appearances and defend himself [...]"[43] The German Criminal Code states in Section 32 (2): "Self-defence means any defensive action which is necessary to avert a present unlawful attack on oneself or another".[44]

Naturally these inputs cannot be transferred directly to international relations. For the assessment of the legality of a state's actions in self-defence only two questions must be answered:

1. What does international law permit the state to do to defend itself?, and 2. What limitation does the state itself set for its defence? Clearly, a nation's interpretation of defence might differ from the generally accepted provisions in public international law, but no nation claiming to be law-abiding can go beyond the recognised authorities of international law (Ipsen 2009: 267).

---

42   Palmer v R, (1971) AC 814; approved in R v McInnes, 55 Cr App R 551, quoted from The Crown Prosecution Service, www.cps.gov.uk/legal-guidance/self-defence-and-prevention-crime, accessed on 14-09-2019.

43   Supreme Court of Colorado 1964), The people of the State of Colorado, Plaintiff in Error, v. Charles E. la Voie, Defendant in Error, 395 P.2d 1001 (1964), quoted from Justia US Law, www.law.justia.com/cases/colorado/supreme-court/1964/20899.html, accessed on 15-09-2019.

44   "Notwehr ist die Verteidigung, die erforderlich ist, um einen gegenwärtigen rechtswidrigen Angriff von sich oder einem anderen abzuwenden." (German Criminal Code (Strafgesetzbuch), §32 (2), quoted from dejure.org, www.dejure.org/gesetze/StGB/32.html, accessed on 14-09-2019. The English translation provided by the Federal Office of Justice is available at https://www.gesetze-im-internet.de/englisch_stgb/englisch_stgb.html#p0186, accessed on 14-09-2019).

To approach these two questions, first the codification of defence in public international law will be discussed, before two examples of rather restrictive national interpretations, the German and the Japanese regulations, will be described.

3.1.1 Public International Law

For most of human history, war was a more or less accepted form of dispute settlement. In the 17th century, the Dutch philosopher Hugo Grotius identified three 'just' causes of war,[45] and the understanding of what a just war is has evolved over time.[46] Defence has always been widely accepted as one of those justifications, but it is not the only one. One vivid example of a just or legal war that was not waged for reasons of defence is the liberation of Kuwait from Iraqi occupation in 1991. The defence of Kuwait had failed in 1990 and the country's territorial integrity had to be restored by the US-led coalition, legitimized by UN Security Council Resolution 678.

This paper does not strive to present a complete treatise on the *ius ad bellum*; for the questions at hand it suffices to conclude that self-defence and collective defence have been accepted as 'just' over the centuries, from the days of Grotius to the 1928 General Treaty for the Renunciation of War (the 'Kellogg-Briand Pact') (Crawford 2019: 717–718) to the adoption of the Charter of the United Nations in 1945.[47]

---

45 Self-defence, reparation, and punishment (Grotius 1625: 2-1-II). He also provides a whole list of 'unjust' reasons for war (Grotius 1625: 2-2-IV-XVI).
46 For a view from the mid-1980s, see: Tucker 1985: 26. However, the understanding has changed significantly even since then. Nevertheless, a general discussion of what would be a "just war" today lays outside of the scope of this paper.
47 The qualification of the right of self-defence as 'inherent' in Article 51 of the United Nations Charter can be understood as referring to pre-existing customary law. Proponents of the legality of anticipatory self-defence use this reference to customary law as an argument (Crawford 2019: 721, 723). It can also be interpreted as indicating that Article 51 only

However, the contemporary understanding of defence in public international law warrants some further explanation.

The UN Charter remains the basis for codified international law, and as one of its cornerstones Article 2(4) bans the unilateral threat or use of force by states except in certain limited circumstances (Crawford 2019: 719):

> All Members shall refrain in their international relations from the threat or use of force against the territorial integrity or political independence of any state, or in any other manner inconsistent with the Purposes of the United Nations. (Crawford 2019: 719)

Of course the wording leaves room for interpretation and the exact meaning of each of its words can be discussed at length. Without attempting an exhaustive legal assessment of the Charter, some details of the generally accepted interpretation are important for the discussion of the limitations of defence. Even if international law evolves with the actions of states (Shaw 2017: 60–63), it provides a frame for policies and the development of strategy.

The prevailing interpretation of Article 2(4) limits the scope of the term 'force' to armed force, employed directly by a state or through proxies.[48] The interpretation of 'threat' remains difficult. Nations will have to tolerate a certain threat of force that is unavoidable when states prepare for self-defence, and threat in the form of deterrence is an accepted means of settling or supressing conflict (Crawford 2019: 720).[49] The phrase 'against the territorial integrity or political

---

adds some provisions to customary law, but does not replace it. This weakens the legal position of the Charter as a whole (Ipsen 2009: 268).

48   It does not include political or economic coercion (Crawford 2019: 720); however,such actions are contrary to the United Nations Charter (Shaw 2017: 855–856).

49   The mere possession of nuclear weapons, for instance, was ruled lawful as long as their threat of use does not contradict the purposes of the United Nations. (Shaw 2017: 856–857).

independence' is widely recognised as having a wide scope, reinforc-
ing and not limiting the previous clause (Crawford 2019: 720; Shaw
2017: 859–860).

The most prominent qualification to the prohibition on the use of
force derives from Article 51 of the Charter, acknowledging self-defence as a category of force[50] for states to act upon in compliance
with international law:

> Nothing in the present Charter shall impair the inherent right
> of individual or collective self-defence if an armed attack occurs
> against a Member of the United Nations, until the Security
> Council has taken measures necessary to maintain international
> peace and security [...] (United Nations 1945: Art. 51)

In this article the term 'armed attack' poses the greatest challenge
for interpretation. Technically speaking, an armed attack is a purposeful action with a certain means in order to inflict damage on a
designated target (Ipsen 2009: 269).

Concerning the purposeful action, the required level of involvement of a state in the attack is disputed. Even assistance, such as
the provision of arms or supplies, could amount to a 'threat or use
of force' or unlawful intervention and thus be prohibited by Article
2(4) of the Charter. And yet such an assistance might fall short of an
'armed attack' justifying individual or collective self-defence, even
though the action in question may be prohibited by the Charter.

This discussion is particularly important in the context of defence
against terrorism (Crawford 2019: 721–722).[51] In its original official ex-

---

50 The other two recognised categories are retorsion and reprisal (Shaw
    2017: 859–860).
51 Until 2001 the interpretation of state involvement in actions of inde-
    pendent non-state actors authorising self-defence was very restricted.
    Since then state practice has evolved, but this does not yet constitute
    a shift in customary international law (Crawford 2019: 745; Ipsen 2009:
    271).

planation of the North Atlantic Treaty text, the US Senate specified that 'armed attack' does not "mean an incident created by irresponsible groups or individuals, but rather an attack by one state upon another."[52] This view has obviously changed after 9/11, but still it is widely accepted that a certain level of intensity is required to justify the term 'attack' (Crawford 2019: 721). Despite contrary ruling of the International Court of Justice, the development of customary law indicates that if this level of intensity is reached, also non-state actors can trigger the self-defence provisions of Article 51 (Ipsen 2009: 271).[53]

The means of the attack are not a decisive factor; they can range from conventional forces to cyber assets or proxy forces (Crawford 2019: 721).

Another important legal discussion concerns the scope of self-defence with respect to anticipatory or pre-emptive self-defence. Proponents of the legality of anticipatory self-defence mostly make their case by referring to customary law.[54] On the other hand, the wording, the situation of the world when the Charter was written in 1945, the ruling of the International Court of Justice,[55] and the expressed positions of nations after 1945[56] rather suggest a restrictive interpre-

---

52 US Department of State (1957), American Foreign Policy 1950–1955, basic documents, Vol I, 6446, p. 835 (cited in Ipsen 2009: 270).
53 NATO's decision to invoke Article 5 of the North Atlantic Treaty (which refers directly to Article 51 of the UN Charter) in a response to the attacks of 9/11 was one of the main reasons that led to the evolution of this view.
54 Such as developed from the 'Caroline Case' and as mentioned in footnote 53 above (Crawford 2019: 723–724). See also Grotius 1625: 2-1-VXI: "Public powers have not only the right of self-defense but also the right to exact punishment. Hence for them it is permissible to forestall an act of violence, which is not immediate, but which is seen to be threatening from a distance; not directly for that, as we have shown, would work injustice but indirectly, by inflicting punishment for a wrong action commenced but not yet carried through."
55 I.e. the 'Armed Activities' ruling (Crawford 2019: 725).
56 Such as in the unanimous condemnation of an Israeli attack on an Iraqi nuclear reactor in 1981 through Security Council Resolution 487 (Crawford 2019: 724).

tation of Article 51, allowing self-defence only in response to an attack that is occurring or reasonably and evidentially perceived to be imminent (Shaw 2017: 866–867). This majority view has not changed after the 'Bush doctrine' that extended the understanding of anticipatory self-defence to less than imminent cases.[57]

Through Article 39 of the Charter, the Security Council "shall determine the existence of any threat to the peace, breach of the peace, or act of aggression" (United Nations 1945: Art. 39) in order to decide on appropriate action. This allows an engagement of the Security Council even short of the 'use of force' defined in Article 2, which would authorise self-defence. A possible albeit unbinding definition of what constitutes an 'act of aggression' was agreed by the United Nations General Assembly in 1974 and subsequently repeated and amended (Crawford 2019: 735–736; Shaw 2017: 855).

3.1.2 Defence in the German 'Grundgesetz'

The original constitution of the Federal Republic of Germany of 1949 was void of any thoughts of military defence and relied purely on the potential membership in a system of collective security (Deutscher Bundestag und Bundesarchiv 1981: 207). In 1954 provisions and responsibilities with respect to a—newly developing—German military were added. This explicitly included a purely defensive purpose of the army. During the Cold War this defensive principle remained visible in leadership, concepts, doctrine, training and education, and equipment (Apel 1979: 30–33).

---

57 Even the official US justification of the attack on Iraq in 2003 did not make a case for anticipatory self-defence but was based on enforcing Security Council resolutions. However, US administrations have maintained a discrepant position on use of force, implied consent to use of force and targeted killings, partly supported by the United Kingdom and other nations (Crawford 2019: 725; Shaw 2017: 868).

However, what constitutes 'defence' is not explicitly defined by the German constitution, but rather referred to the interpretation of international humanitarian law (Weinheimer 2006: 4).[58]

Until 1994 the employment of the military for defence was restricted to the *Verteidigungsfall*, the declared state of defence—"the federal territory is under attack by armed force or imminently threatened with such an attack" (Basic Law for the Federal Republic of Germany, Article 115a (1))—or to subsidiary help "in order to avert an imminent danger to the existence or free democratic basic order of the Federation or of a Land" (Basic Law for the Federal Republic of Germany, Article 87a (4); Ipsen 2009: 273).[59] Rulings of the Constitutional Court beginning in 1994 and following interpretations of Article 25, which incorporates general principles of international law—such as the right to individual and collective defence from Article 51 of the UN Charter—into German legislation superseding federal law, allowed for a wider interpretation of defence (Ipsen 2009: 274).[60]

Clearly, when the provisions for the state of defence with the authorization of far reaching measures, including the use of military force, were introduced into the *Grundgesetz* in 1968, it was unthinkable that a similar magnitude of impact and necessary reaction could stem from international non-state actors employing asymmetric means or weapons of mass destruction. The change in threat was widely recognised and incorporated into government policy in the German White Paper of 1994 (Weinheimer 2006: 4).

---

58 Opinions that indeed the Grundgesetz sets a narrower margin to what defence is than international law have been discussed but largely discarded (Ipsen 2009: 267).

59 Employment of military means, for example for counter-mine operations or humanitarian aid, had to be based directly on international law and could not refer to the German constitution or the North Atlantic Treaty (Giermann 1991: 396).

60 A similiar argumentation can already be found in Bülow 1984: 62–63. However, this work also included more restrictive views (Bülow 1984: 27–31).

However, the constitution was not changed, and attempts to define at least certain aspects of the employment of the military for defence outside of the state of defence led to fierce political and juristic discussions, but eventually failed. In moments of crisis, decision-makers from the fighter pilot up to the Minister of Defence, remain without clear legal guidance.[61]

Organisationally and with a view to training and cooperation, the German federal and Länder administrations have taken important steps for improved—subsidiary and legal—military support in cases of civilian defence and emergencies.

An important point of discussion is the scope of what the German military is to defend. Collective defence to the benefit of other nations is widely accepted, but the understanding of what the Federal Republic of Germany itself comprises differs. The traditional interpretation was narrow and based on the constitutional wording only required the Bundeswehr to deter violence and secure the territorial integrity should an aggressor disturb the peace (Apel 1979: 24). Against the backdrop of globalization, cyberspace, and irregular warfare, the appropriateness of this interpretation is increasingly questioned, but still the mere suggestion that the Bundeswehr might also have to defend German security interests such as commercial shipping routes led to the resignation of Federal President Köhler in 2010 (ARD 2010).

3.1.3 Article 9 of the Japanese Constitution

A similar discussion is taking place in Japan, albeit within maybe even narrower boundaries than the debate in Germany. Article 9 of the Japanese constitution strictly restricts the establishment and

---

61   This is illustrated by the discussions and eventual Constitutional Court ruling concerning the 'Luftsicherheitsgesetz' (airspace security law) (Weinheimer 2006: 5, court ruling: Federal Constitutional Court (Bundesverfassungsgericht), Judgment of the First Senate of 15 February 2006 - 1 BvR 357/05 -, paras. 1-156).

employment of Japanese armed forces.[62] The long-held interpretation of this 'minimum self-defence' as only allowing for individual, but not collective self-defence has slowly been widened. In 2001 Japan provided logistical support to the US Navy during their attacks on Afghanistan, and in 2004 ground forces were deployed to Iraq as part of the coalition against Saddam Hussein (Sebata 2007: 146–147).[63] The Japanese constitution has not been amended; only the interpretation of Article 9 has evolved under the current and the previous administration. This is not only a consequence of an increased direct threat to Japan—this could have been reacted to within the narrower interpretation[64]—but rather of a fear of abandonment by the US, the senior partner in their alliance and guarantor of Japan's security (Sebata 2007: 152–154).

This development is interesting for two particular reasons. First the Japanese Self Defence Forces are losing more and more of their structural inability to attack. The status of a state's security services is important, as can be observed in Kosovo, where the political

---

62 "Renunciation of war: Article 9: Aspiring sincerely to an international peace based on justice and order, the Japanese people forever renounce war as a sovereign right of the nation and the threat or use of force as means of settling international disputes. In order to accomplish the aim of the preceding paragraph, land, sea, and air forces, as well as other war potential, will never be maintained. The right of belligerency of the state will not be recognized." (Japanese Constitution 1947).

63 The article (Sebata 2007) provides a very theory-based view on Japanese policies.

64 And also the development towards collective self-defence started with the increase of Chinese-Japanese tensions in 2012 (Sebata 2007: 145; Hardy, James 2014: 34–35). The strict verbal interpretation of the US-imposed constitution had been softened multiple times over the course of the Cold War, in connection with the Korean War and Japan's increasing global interests. (A comprehensive overview is provided by Ito 2006: 195–214, 284–289, although his description and interpretation is clearly biased through his personal engagement for a pacifistic Japanese constitution).

leadership has risked severe disputes with its international sup-porters over the transformation of its Kosovo Security Forces into full-fledged Kosovo Armed Forces. A similar transformation of the Japanese armed forces could lead to new, and possibly unintended, developments in the security dynamics of the region characterised by territorial conflicts between Japan and Russia, China, and South Korea, respectively, a struggle for control over the East and South China Sea and the threat by North Korea (Hardy 2014: 38).

Secondly, it could be a very indirect, almost mercantilist approach to defence as a continuation of bandwagoning: Investing in and em-ploying military capabilities and widening the interpretation of the constitution to include collective self-defence do not in the first place serve Japan's security directly, but prove its value to the superior mil-itary power in the partnership. Given the extraordinary geostrategic importance of Japan, the fear of complete US abandonment is prob-ably not warranted,[65] but deeper military cooperation certainly con-tributes to the defence of Japan.

3.1.4 Legality and Legitimacy of Defence

The first legal discussions of defence referred to international law. This implies an obvious, but nevertheless important fact: in interna-tional relations, defence only occurs where international law is ap-plicable. So regardless of the individual interpretations of the pro-visions, any situation where all aspects of an armed attack remain within one state and thus within its jurisdiction is not subject to in-ternational law and neither the concepts of self-defence in general nor the provisions of Articles 2 or 51 of the UN Charter are applicable (Ipsen 2009: 269; Shaw 2017: 857).[66]

---

65 Albeit historically present (Sebata 2007: 166).
66 Naturally this does not preclude the applicability of other provisions, such as human rights or possibilities to intervene on the basis of Chapter VII of the Charter.

Discussing the specific wording might appear tiresome, but legal provisions concerning defence only make sense as long as the content of the provisions is not so wide and variable that virtually everything can be included in the definition (Ipsen 2009: 266). There is no clearly defined, neat outer limit of what defence is, but as a rule of thumb it can be concluded that the further the limit is stretched, the smaller is the legitimacy of any defensive action.

The importance of legitimacy for political decisions and strategies, particularly for alliances, goes back to Thucydides' times (Koliopoulos/Platias 1956: 72–73) and will be reflected later in this paper.

Defence is not only a question of legality or political legitimation. Soldiers of free and democratic nations who are confronted with death or required to kill deserve and need a steadfast moral basis that can only come from self-defence or the defence of others. This provides secure footing for decisions, but morally limits the room of political manoeuvre: operations must be limited to actors violently disturbing the peace; neither annihilation nor occupation can be the goal, but only a just return to peace; means employed must be proportionate to the goal; and humanity must not be replaced by hate (de Maizière 1993: 463).

The UN Charter is quite firm in establishing the legal side of a monopoly on the legitimate use of physical force on behalf of the United Nations, however, a complete monopoly also requires a factual element. This would mean a concentration of instruments of physical power in the hands of the authority responsible for securing or restoring the peace. Currently, this is certainly not the case for the United Nations, which relies on its members to enforce and employ their respective monopolies on force for the aims and provisions of the Charter (Ipsen 2009: 268). This leads to a situation where international law obliges states to only react as a first responder until the police arrive. Only the police might never come, or if they do, they might bring neither gun nor baton. This is particularly difficult for members of an Alliance that seeks security through a rules-based international order on the basis of the UN Charter. Enhancing the power and vigour of the United Nations would therefore benefit the security of NATO—as long as no permanent member of the Security Council is the source or benefactor of the threat.

3.2 Strategic Concepts and Theories

The final area to be discussed after the views on historical examples and on NATO in particular, and the judicial perspective, is the field of strategic thinking as such. The list of famous thinkers that worried about war and peace is endless. It includes Sun Tzu, Antoine-Henri Jomini, and Carl von Clausewitz from a military strategic point of view; philosophers like Augustine, Thomas Hobbes, and Immanuel Kant, scholars of political science like Samuel Huntington, Francis Fukuyama, and Stephen Walt, and certainly also practitioners like Friedrich II., Winston Churchill, and Henry Kissinger.

This eclectic mix of writers from a variety of backgrounds demonstrates the breadth of possible avenues of approach to the great questions of war and peace, including to what defence is. This section will briefly describe and discuss some traditional and modern features of strategic thinking that were deemed important for the question at hand.

3.2.1 Defence and Deterrence

The idea of deterrence is to prevent an attack through influencing the adversary's decision making by increasing the foreseeable costs or the risks of an aggression.[67]

Deterrence is an integral part of military strategy. Its importance increased with the development of weapons that make defence and war in general unthinkable (Schelling 1966: 2–5). Bernard Brodie recognised early that in the age of the atomic bomb the focus of the military has to shift: "Thus far the chief purpose of [the US] military

---

67 To discuss, or even present, the different definitions and features of deterrence would be far beyond the scope of this study. For a recent and concise overview of relevant concepts see: Mazarr 2018.

establishment has been to win wars. From now on its chief purpose must be to avert them." (Brodie 1946: 76).[68]

The logical consequence could be a decreasing importance of defence. However, deterrence and defence do not co-exist in an either-or-relationship. Most obvious is the blurred line between the two terms in the model of 'deterrence by denial'. An effective defence is intended to raise the stakes for the adversary, forcing them to employ more means to overcome it and achieve their aims. A missile defence system is a typical example. It is only operational when the radars are activated and the launchers ready to engage. At the same time a sufficiently advanced system by its very existence deters adversaries from even trying to overcome it. Thus, in order to avoid an overlap of the two concepts, one would have to draw the line between deterrence and defence at the moment an intercepting missile is released in the case of an attack. That would be a narrower understanding than that suggested by the definitions cited in the introduction and current Headquarters practice. Arguably, an active missile defence system deters and defends at the same time.

The distinction is even more complex in the new domain of cyberspace. Here defence is taking place continuously and is even required to demonstrate a nation's defensive capabilities.[69]

For NATO 'deterrence and defence' is a fixed term that is traditionally understood as a sequence: First, deterrence takes place, and when deterrence fails, defence comes into play. This is, however, an understanding that does not sufficiently reflect the overlapping relationship between the two.

Additionally, developments in the strategic environment lead to threats that are very hard—or even impossible—to deter. This in-

---

68 However, his assessment that an atomic war would have no winner was disputed, not least within the Kennedy administration (Magenheimer 1986: 13-15).

69 For a comprehensive analysis of deterrence in cyberspace (in German) and proposals for the development of new deterrence approaches see: Hoberg 2019).

cludes terrorists or other actors employing means that are difficult to attribute, such as cyber or covert operations. Here swift, direct defence is required, 24/7.

Another relation between deterrence and defence arises from the description of the deterrent. Deterrence measures can be taken only for the sake of deterrence. This is obviously the case for the installation of a second strike capability ensuring mutual nuclear destruction. But deterrence measures can also comprise visible or suspected defensive measures, most evidently in the concepts of deterrence by denial.

For the soldier this distinction might not be critical, but in a political Alliance it must be clearly understood that the same defensive measure can serve both defence and deterrence.

The third relationship is the defence against deterrence. Here resilience has a role to play as will be discussed later, but also measures such as the active promotion of cohesion, strategic communication, and reconnaissance efforts. The attacker has the natural advantage to be able to decide about location, time, and kind of the attack, but if the defender has sufficient information about the aggressor's plan, about half of the attacker's advantage is gone (Blum 1987: 259).

In one respect deterrence is difficult for policymakers and soldiers alike: It cannot be measured or quantified, and not even its success can be proven. Did the adversary not attack because they were deterred or did they choose not to attack for some other reason? Insufficient deterrence becomes only apparent when it is too late, when it has failed. Deterrence therefore is an object of faith (Tucker 1985: 17) and by its very nature not satisfying especially when it comes to existential questions of national or Alliance security. To overcome these doubts, the Reagan administration tried to exploit the overlap of deterrence by denial and defence with its Strategic Defence Initiative (SDI) (Tucker 1985: 100–105). But in addition to the challenges for the weapons control regime of the time, it carried the same flaw as the previous deterrence approach. Whether or not a system like SDI worked and sufficiently protected the United States would only have become clear once a nuclear war had started,[70] and until then the Allies would have had to remain dependent on their faith in American protection.

The different concepts of deterrence evolve continuously and maintain their importance also in view of the modern interpretation of international relations.[71] A newer possible deterrent, applicable in traditional scenarios as well as against hybrid or terrorist threats is the preparedness of a nation in terms of consequence management (Major/Mölling 2015: 4). This could also be considered part of—in this case mostly civil—defence. It also touches on the relationship between defence and resilience.

3.2.2 Defence and Resilience

When Generaloberst von Seeckt discussed "Landesverteidigung" (national defence) in 1930, he freely admitted this term to be more political than military (Seeckt 1930: 17). He came to this conclusion shortly before he happened to become a politician as Member of Parliament, but the judgement is certainly even truer today than it was during his lifetime. Von Seeckt, picking up Clausewitz's thinking, identified the will to resist and survive as crucial for defence (Seeckt 1930: 10). Since then the overlap between civilian and military defence has grown considerably.

For alliances this overlap poses a challenge, as hybrid security policy rests primarily with the individual nations since most measures must be taken on the national or regional level. At the same time many

---

70 Successful protection would have been unlikely: Tucker 1985: 103. Even 35 years later defence against intercontinental ballistic missiles remains technologically extremely challenging and does not offer solutions for submarine-launched missiles at a relative short distance or propelled, 'smart' missiles.

71 For example, deterrence is relevant across what the US Joint Chiefs of Defence call the competition continuum: US Joint Chiefs of Staff 2019: vii, 10–11. A discussion of the competition continuum can be found in section 3.2.5 (Contest) of this paper.

nations do not possess sufficient means to do so (Major/Mölling 2015: 4). Additionally, suppliers of water, energy, financial services etc. are often privately owned and have little interest in measures that increase resilience, but do not provide profit (Major/Mölling 2015: 3).

If measures like missile defence systems are part of a deterrence by denial approach or active defence, then resilience can be understood as passive defence or deterrence (Lambert 2002: 44),[72] in the form of 'deterrence by denial of effectiveness'. Understood in this form resilience would also have a deterrent effect against non-state threats such as terrorism or covert operations (Lambert 2002: 43–44). If an action is not likely to have any major impact because of the preparations of the defender, the aggressor is less likely to undertake the attack or an opponent's deterrence by punishment is less effective. However, at least in Germany, civil defence is not intended to have a deterrent effect. Preparations follow only the established risk analysis pattern indicating the likelihood of an event and the magnitude of the possible damage inflicted by it (Ehrhart/Neuneck 2016: 2–6).

An active form of resilience would involve border protection and functioning control mechanisms in both the private sector and the media. This would offer protection against infiltration and measures to undermine the stability of a state (Major/Mölling 2015: 4).

Additionally measures for better protection of basic functions against all sort of damage, including catastrophic accidents, natural desasters or—obviously—pandemics is required and can be part of defence or preparation of defence. Several NATO exercises had to

---

72 Lambert's attribution of resilience to deterrence could be caused by the author's use of his native language French, where the term used for 'deterrence' is 'dissuasion', allowing for a slightly wider scope of interpretation. Without delving into linguistics, one could describe the French term ‚dissuasion' as a combination of the English 'deterrence' and 'dissuasion'. A similar semantic difference exists in Russian. The word for Western 'deterrence' has a more aggressive connotation, whereas the word for Soviet/Russian deterrence rather suggests a defensive attitude (Tiedtke 1986: 26–27).

be canceled because of fear of infections and an aircraft carrier rendered useless by a virus is a strategic asset missing for posture, messaging and possibly fighting.

COVID-19 also revealed to what extent some societies rely on military support in times of crisis. This necessary support must not jeopardize the militaries' capability to discharge their defence duties. The pandemic was—and still is—a pressure test for societies and their militaries. Friend and foe will notice the way they perform, show tenacity, and retain their ability to act. The result can be a deterrent effect—or an invitation to exploit weaknesses.

A security policy focussed on systemic vulnerabilities and coordinating the relationship of deterrence, resilience, and defence could considerably improve the security in NATO and the EU (Major/Mölling 2015: 1).

3.2.3 The Security Dilemma

A security dilemma exists when "many of the means by which a state tries to increase its security decrease the security of others." (Jervis 1978: 169). Even when so called status-quo states focus only on stability, actions like armament or capability development taken to increase their own security will decrease at least the perceived security of other states. Due to the largely anarchic structure of the international system, these other states will react by increasing their security. They can do this defensively, by arming themselves and thus triggering a security spiral like an arms race, or they can react aggressively by trying to decrease the other state's power, initiating immediate conflict (Wivel 2011: 2389). Naturally, there are limitations to the model, such as 'security communities' or generally situations where it is impossible to clearly define or name an adversary (Booth/Wheeler 1987: 316–317).

In his considerations concerning the security dilemma, Jervis describes four scenarios, four possible worlds influencing the danger emanating from the security dilemma. For him the decisive variables are the degree to which a state's or an alliance's posture is recognisably offensive or defensive, and the current development of warfare,

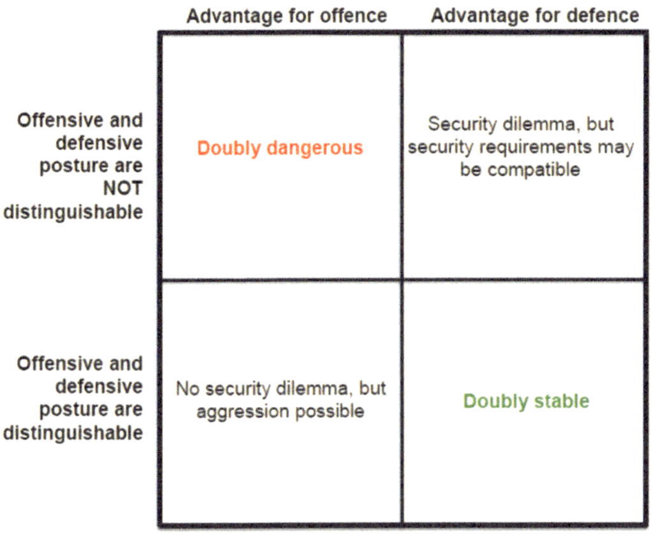

	Advantage for offence	Advantage for defence
Offensive and defensive posture are NOT distinguishable	**Doubly dangerous**	Security dilemma, but security requirements may be compatible
Offensive and defensive posture are distinguishable	No security dilemma, but aggression possible	**Doubly stable**

Fig. 1: The four worlds in the security delemma (own figure based on Jervis 1978: 211).

i.e. as to whether technology, deployment, doctrine etc. rather favour the offence or the defence. That leads him to four levels of danger, or stability, respectively, depicted in figure 1.

Although the concept of the security dilemma has been widely discussed, criticised, and expanded since its development, it is generally recognised as one of the most prominent models to describe international relations (Glaser 1997: 172–173),[73] with the intensity of the dilemmas varying over time and space (Wivel 2011: 2389).

Naturally, the awareness of the security dilemma must not lead to blurred or naïve interpretations of intelligence or judgements of another actor's behaviour. The—failed—British attempts to appease Hitler before World War II were partly caused by the assumption that

73 Also Shiping Tang is pointing out that realists argue within the security dilemma, while other schools of thought try to alleviate or dissolve it (Tang 2009: 587–588).

Hitler sought only the rectification of legitimate and limited grievances and by the intention to avoid 'unnecessary' conflict of the kind that had triggered World War I (Jervis 1978: 183). One of the most important criticisms of the security dilemma model is the fact that it fails to recognise the existence of 'greedy' states (Glaser 1997: 174).

NATO's first phase was marked by two superpowers and their respective alliances living in a security dilemma.[74] This led to the approaches of deterrence and later disarmament, both of which are empirically and theoretically viable responses to a security dilemma (Wirtz 2005: 387).

A related problem is the burden of responsibility that comes with increased and expanded power. In Robert Jervis' further explanation and development of John Herz' original idea of a security dilemma, the author uses a quote from the former British Prime Minister Arthur James Balfour to illustrate how an expansion of power also entails an expansion of responsibility:

> Every time I come to a discussion—at intervals of, say, five years—I find there is a new sphere which we have got to guard, which is supposed to protect the gateways of India. Those gateways are getting further and further away from India, and I do not know how far west they are going to be brought by the General Staff.[75]

This explains the responsibility dilemma the US and NATO face in Afghanistan today. After the Article 5 support in the wake of the 9/11 attacks, the US and the Alliance helped remove the Taliban regime and set out to bring stability and security to the country. This was first attempted with a limited engagement in Kabul. When that proved to be insufficient, NATO took over control—and responsibility—of the whole country. Officially the responsibility for security was returned to the Afghan government with the shift from the International Sup-

---

74 The concept was developed in Herz 1950: 157.
75 Arthur James Balfour, quoted in Jervis 1978: 169.

port Mission to Afghanistan (ISAF) to the Resolute Support Mission (RSM) in 2014, but still the US and NATO are struggling to enable the Afghan government to exercise its control and provide security.

NATO should be careful to project power in order to defend before a threat materialises and in the process willingly or unwillingly take over responsibility. In this respect, NATO's latest engagement in Iraq could be a strategic mistake. NATO, with all its members, is part of the coalition to defeat ISIS, but has only supported the efforts in the region with limited AWACS resources and some personnel in coordination and liaison functions as part of the NATO Training Mission in Iraq (NTM-I). The fighting and the training of the Iraqi forces conducted by the Allies was initially based on bilateral or multilateral agreements with Iraq and/or the US. With the introduction of the NATO Mission in Iraq and the Alliance taking charge of training and advising (through re-flagging or newly deployed forces), NATO is now a much more tangible actor. On the one hand this may lead to direct opposition from the antagonist, but on the other hand, according to the responsibility dilemma, it may also result in an increased responsibility of a visible, powerful actor in and for a highly volatile region. That would likely be a responsibility NATO never intended to assume.

It is important to take into account the responsibility dilemma when judging the contribution of the task of 'Projecting Stability' to the defence of the Alliance.

3.2.4 Political Warfare, Defensive Defence, and Similar Concepts

Apart from the classical theories of defence, there are also completely different and decisively un-military concepts of defence. These include 'political warfare', a concept denying the utility of war as a means of defence. Superior values and ideas are to conquer the world and will, if necessary, endure and prevail should a violent, militarily unopposed occupation take place.[76] Hart appreciates these argu-

---

76 Concept of political warfare of Stephen King-Hall, described in Hart 1955: 254–257; Ebert 1981: 25.

ments, but recognises that this concept is unlikely to be tested by any nation (Hart 1955: 254), and while this assessment is probably as true today as it was in 1955, it foreshadows the modern "fight for the hearts and minds", the constant struggle in press-conferences and social media and TV-stations and support to political parties being employed as hybrid warfare means.

Defensive Defence calls for a military defence limited to one's own territory, using and enhancing the depth and advantages of the country and demonstrating the absence of aggressive intentions by the armed forces' structural inability to attack (Afheldt 1984: 18–21; Goblirsch 1984: 131–135). Long-term defensive preparations, such as reforestation of possible avenues of attack, are unlikely to be seen as provocative (Blum 1987: 259). The concept was developed to overcome the security dilemma based on the idea of undermining Russian propaganda and thus the will of the communist satellite states to support Russia in a war against the West.[77] Apart from the fact that these potentially fragile members of an opposing Alliance are now NATO Allies, modern developments in technology and warfare contradict a tendency to Defensive Defence.[78] Also, today's Alliance geography requires mobile and flexible forces, as do the current tasks of projecting stability and fight against terrorism.

In academic discussions these approaches certainly merit attention as they offer an answer to the security dilemma. There are two major limitations though. First, and that is recognized even by the proponents of these approaches, they largely aim at preventing a classic invasion and occupation of territory (Ebert 1981: 30). They remain part of the thinking of the first age of NATO.

---

[77] The proposed concept was to aim at the will of the communist satellite states to support Russia in a war against the West (Afhledt 1984: 24–27).

[78] NATO (2018), Framework for future alliance operations. 2018 report, NATO, www.act.nato.int/images/stories/media/doclibrary/180514_ffao18. pdf, accessed on 07-09-2018, p. 22, 28.

Secondly, in the current situation of NATO, these concepts do not provide the feeling of security or protection of interests sought by the Allies.

For some nations, particularly in the Baltics, there is just not enough space to conduct Defensive Defence. Given their historical experiences and geostrategic realities, guerrilla warfare—and to some extend Social Defence—is an obvious part of their strategic thinking. However, they did not join NATO to have to rely only on that and suffer through 90 years as a Russian colony until an East European Ghandi leads them peacefully back to freedom.[79]

On the other side of the spectrum, Allies like the US or France have global obligations and interests that certainly could not be protected with either of these concepts. Even in the 1980s a timespan of more than 10 years was deemed necessary for the spread of the thought and further research (Ebert 1981: 27, 179–180).[80] With the conditions for the employment of these concepts not at all improved—and with Machiavelli's suggestion to await attack and fight in your homeland only with a well-armed and stalwart population in mind (Machiavelli 1531: 201)—their application in NATO remains unrealistic.

---

79 And a combination with traditional defence would contradict these concepts' central aim of solving the security dilemma (Ebert 1981: 184).

80 A very vivid example of how unthinkable this alternative school of thought was for American scholars and policymakers can be found in Dunn, Keith/Staudenmaier, William (eds.) (1985), Alternative Military Strategies for the Future, Boulder: London. In the book, the title of which includes both 'alternative' and 'future', former Under Secretary of Defense for Policy Komer provides a foreword for the results of a conference covering the most prominent schools of thought (Dunn/Staudenmaier 1985: 16). Ambassador Komer sets out with his first essential proposition being: "The only realistic aim is to preserve a stable and acceptable balance of power – conventional as well as nuclear." (Komer 1985: xii).

3.2.5 Contest

US strategists have conducted a radical paradigm shift. They have replaced the differences of war and peace, or the slightly more differentiated notion of a peace-crisis-war spectrum that is widely accepted in NATO, with what is called a "competition continuum" (US Joint Chiefs of Staff 2019: v, 1–2). This can have great impact on the understanding of defence, since in a competition continuum, the US is constantly contesting other actors throughout the spectrum of possible international relations. In the explanation of the Joint Chiefs no reference is made to defence. The 'key terms'—formulated very similar to Military Strategic Effects—do not include the verbs 'defend' or 'protect' or the like.[81] The word defence (or defense) is virtually absent in the paper.[82]

The underlying thought of the competition continuum is an understanding of the world as an arena of competition with states and non-state actors seeking to protect and advance their own interests and continually competing for diplomatic, economic, and strategic advantage. This competition is described as being conducted through a mixture of cooperation, competition below armed conflict, and armed conflict. It is considered to pertain to diplomatic, informational, military, and economic efforts (US Joint Chiefs of Staff 2019: v, 1–2).

The Joint Chiefs may have a point in observing those three approaches, which form a continuum with an inherent logic. The continuum possibly describes a realistic feature of international relations, but why does it have to replace the categories of peace and

---

81   The list comprises: defeat (adversary), deny (adversary), degrade (adversary), disrupt (adversary), enhance (advantage), manage (advantage), delay (disadvantage), engage selectively (with partner/competitor), maintain (alliance/partnership), advance (relationship) (Joint Chiefs of Staff 2019: 5–6, additions in parenthesis made by the author for clarification).

82   It does appear in seven instances in US Joint Chiefs of Staff 2019: as part of 'Department of Defense', describing the defense partnership with Saudi Arabia, air-defense and acknowledging deterrence (not an element of the competition continuum) as contributing to defence.

war? Clearly defining the threshold between war and peace has become more difficult in times of cyber attacks and hybrid activities, and therefore the conclusion drawn by the Joint Chiefs is that a more nuanced model is required by the current operational environment (US Joint Chiefs of Staff 2019: 1). However, just labelling the whole spectrum 'competition' appears to be rather more simplistic than nuanced. The three elements of cooperation, competition below armed conflict, and armed conflict are not to replace war and peace, but they are to be employed in the competition continuum (US Joint Chiefs of Staff 2019: 4)—just as a multitude of activities has always been allocated to the categories of war and peace.

The competition continuum replaces the objective description of a situation with a label for a relationship between actors, walking back in time across the *limes*.

The threshold between war and peace has many important functions, such as the differentiation between *ius ad bello* and *ius in bellum*. This is partly recognised by the Joint Chiefs of Staff[83], but they claim that geopolitical rivals of the US such as Russia and China exploit the limitations imposed by a clear distinction between war and peace (US Joint Chiefs of Staff 2019: 1–2). However, the distinction clearly remains important for western democracies even if indeed the US' adversaries should not think that way[84]. This concept of the continuum also neglects the importance of international organisations and the rules-based international order. It is an exclusively realistic description of the world that does not demonstrate a desire for and support of, let alone a vision for, peace.[85]

---

83 They also mention the US constitution and domestic law (US Joint Chiefs of Staff 2019: 1).

84 'Our adversaries don't think that way' (General Joseph Dunford, quoted in US Joint Chiefs of Staff 2019: 1).

85 Colin Gray provides an overview of different understandings or levels of peace (absence of war—political peace—absurdity of war) in: Gray 2010: 111–112.

In total, the competition model is not, as was claimed, a new description of international relations, but rather a list of elements being employed in international relations. These elements are certainly of particular importance to the US strategy and they are to be employed to achieve desired strategic objectives (US Joint Chiefs of Staff 2019: 4). The US approach to contesting is already expressed in the Coast Guard's strategy for the Arctic. It aims at "projecting sovereignty" and holding the line against competitors who do not respect the international order (Lamothe 2019).

Explaining international competition by looking back on the Cold War period, the Joint Chiefs refer only to the competition between the superpowers. They refer to examples (achievements in space, medals at the Olympics) applicable only to states. Another example they employ is the competition of states within international organisations (US Joint Chiefs of Staff: 1). None of these descriptors point to an understanding of NATO competing as an alliance. However, contesting could possibly have become strategically more important today and necessary for NATO to apply as well. This will be discussed in the final chapter of this book, but regardless of its potential military strategic value, a strategic approach citing the Great Game of the 19th century as an example (US Joint Chiefs of Staff 2019: 9) is not likely to garner much support in Western European societies.

One practitioner of permanent competition is Israel. The country's policy was very pointedly summarized by Prime Minister Netanyahu in one sentence: "If someone rises up to kill you, kill him first."[86]

This approach had already been practiced over the last decades but was intensified in the summer of 2019. Over the course of a single week, the Israel Defense Forces hit a base in Syria, destroyed a

---

86 Netanjahu, Benjamin (2019) on Twitter.com (https://twitter.com/netanyahu/status/1165377368220942337, 14:36h 24-08-2019, accessed on 09-09-2019): "In a major operational effort, we have thwarted an attack against Israel by the Iranian Quds Force & Shi'ite militias. I reiterate: Iran has no immunity anywhere. Our forces operate in every sector against the Iranian aggression. 'If someone rises up to kill you, kill him first.'"

weapons depot in Iraq, and undertook drone strikes in Lebanon (Cook 2019).

The criticism of this new escalation highlights the risk of the contest approach. The attacks were militarily successful but further enraged Hezbollah fighters and increased the risk of a large-scale attack on Israel (Halbfinger et al. 2019: Sec.A, p.1) even if neither side intends to engage in a full-scale war (Anderson 2019).

3.3 Strategical Analysis

Obviously, despite the efforts of many great minds over the course of millennia, there still is no rulebook or comprehensive manual for strategy, and this paper certainly is no attempt of providing the first chapter. In the following, a theoretical model is introduced to display strategic thinking based on how graphs are used to display mathematical functions. Additionally the graphs depicting strategic thoughts can also be expressed in abstract functions, which can help to bring clarity and precision to a field notorious for its ambiguity and vagueness—thus the designation 'strategical analysis', as in 'mathematical analysis'.

However, this is not to give the impression that strategies can be calculated[87] or that there might be a 'theory of everything' for strategy. The model is merely a tool to improve understanding; the variables used to depict factors cannot easily be given numerical values. It is merely that, a model that is to be employed for further deliberations.

After the model has been described, it will be employed to elaborate on the meaning of defence.

---

87   It is thus a different approach than the attempts of 'defence analysis'. For a sharp critique of that endeavour see: Gray 2010: 189–190.

3.3.1 Introduction of the Model

There is already a multitude of graphic representations for different strategic thoughts. Ends, ways, and means alone have been represented in the literature as pyramids, networks, and even stools.

However, those graphics, and more importantly the underlying thoughts, lack the crucial element of time.[88] Admittedly, the additional dimension adds complexity, but the visualization allows a more focussed discussion and helps in strategy development.

The starting point for understanding the model is the graphic depiction of one strategic issue influencing the security of a state or an alliance over time. To influence the shape of this curve is the goal of a strategy.

Figure 2 depicts the course of the future relationship of an imaginative state A with its peer state actor B. This graph only indicates that the relationship will change over time and that the relationship at any given date results in a certain level of security for state A.

This very simple visualisation already puts into question the widely used notion of an 'end-state' that is to be achieved by a strategy. Where on the time axis would that be placed? What happens to the 'end'-state one day later and what does it say about the time span between today and the chosen point in time? Against this backdrop, the 'end' of a strategy cannot be just one point on the relationship curve (for example, "peace deal signed"), but the 'end' must be an enduring state that is to be aspired (such as "friendly neighbourly relationship").

Equally important as the end is something missing in most strategic models: The definition of what must not happen on the way to the end. A friendly relationship ten years from now is not worth a lot if years 3–8 are marked by brutal war. The graph with those considerations added is shown in figure 3.

---

88 This has been recognised by the US Joint Chiefs of Staff. They have started to pursue a shift from a strategic mindset of 'campaigns' to one of 'campaigning' (US Joint Chiefs of Staff 2019: vi, 4–5). Strategy development over time is more frequently used in economics and controlling.

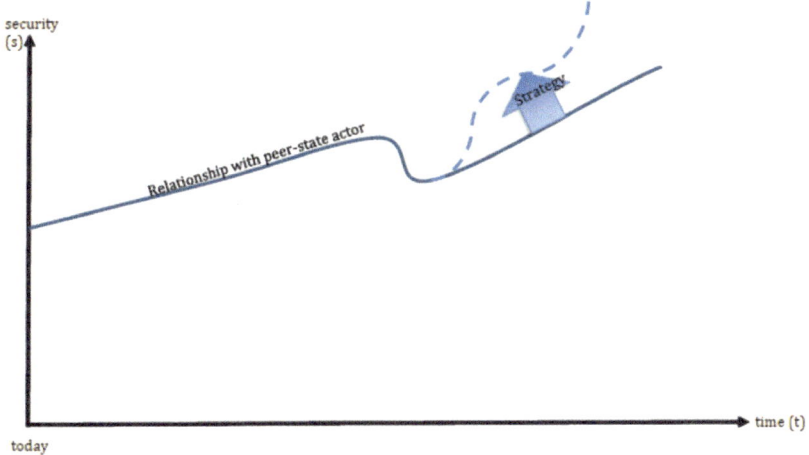

Fig. 2: Example of a function of security over time.

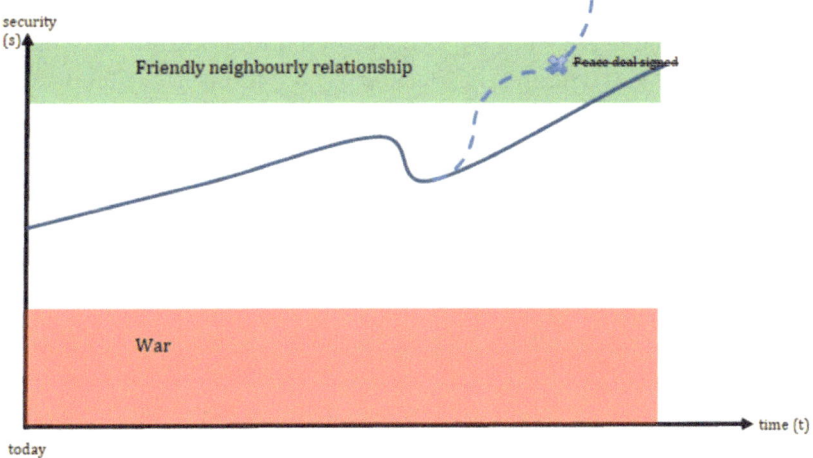

Fig. 3: Considerations for the strategy of an exemplary state.

The strategy of the imaginative state will, for its entire application period, strive for the curve to move into the green zone and to avoid the red zone.

The US competition continuum would add the idea to the model that the total amount of security is limited, i.e. that by trying to move the curve up, each state tries to increase its share of security.

63

In order to further operationalise the model, abstract labelling must be used (fig. 4)

The shape of curve f(t) is influenced by different variables. In a state-to-state relationship these can include economic cooperation, possible border disputes, or migration issues, financial support, bilateral agreements, etc. Some of these variables have more weight than others. So a function of security over time could look like this:

$$f(t) = a * b2 * c * 2d$$

Some of the variables can be intentionally influenced, others not.It may also be part of a strategy to add new variables. Which variables can be worked with depends on the scope of the strategy. A military strategy will be able to address fewer variables than a 'grand' strategy and the strategy of a ministry of the interior will aim at different variables than that pursued by a coordinator of humanitarian aid. Should a function be defined only by variables that cannot be influenced, it can be disregarded—the respective strategic issue is part of the strategic environment, and therefore cannot be an object of strategy.

The variables could be broken down further, depending on the level on which the strategy is to be used. The composition of the variables will encompass the ways and means of the strategy chosen to positively influence the shape of the curve. This influence will be limited by the availability of resources, requiring a first step of prioritisation.

Evidently, the strategic environment consists of more than one strategic issue, and thus the model cannot have only one curve. However, it is not necessary to introduce a multitude of functions for all thinkable scenarios. To understand the mechanisms and interdependencies between the functions it is sufficient to continue with three curves representing three different strategic issues. These can span military strategic themes .but could also come from different areas of concern. A strategic issue can be anything that influences

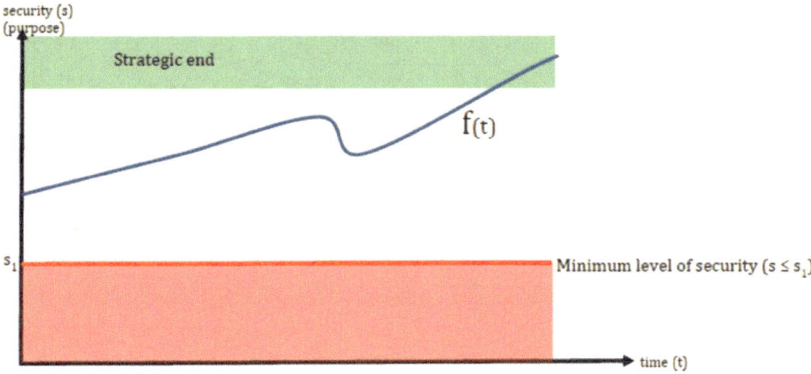

Fig. 4: Abstract depiction of the function of one strategic issue.

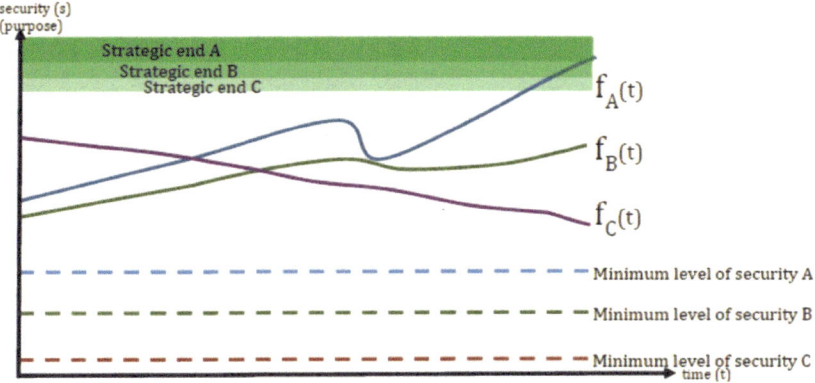

Fig. 5: The strategic environment is represented by three functions within the model.

the security of a state over time,[89] from a military threat to climate change.

An important point to note is that a different minimum level of security is defined for each of the functions and that each function aims for a specific strategic end.

---

89   For a security strategy.

The three curves could be described with the following functions:

$$fA(t) = a * b2 * c * 2d; \quad fB(t) = e * f * g + 2e; \quad fC(t) = h * c * i - e$$

Some variables may influence only one function, some more than one; and some may even influence one curve positively and another negatively. These variables express strategic problems or even dilemmas requiring the strategist's attention and decisions of prioritisation. This way constellations such as a security dilemma can be easily visualised.

This depiction of strategic thinking demonstrates the art and the aim of any strategy:

$$\int f_A(t) + f_B(t) + f_C(t) \rightarrow \max ! \text{ and } f_A(t) > s_A; f_B(t) > s_B; f_C(t) > s_C$$

The aim of any strategy must be to maximise the area under all the curves, i.e. to influence each of the strategic issues in such a way as to produce as much security as possible. At the same time none of the curves must fall under its respective minimum level of security.

Without question, this general model is a simplification and does not cover all the details[90] and interdependencies. It also lacks some precision in the mathematical expression, for example with regard to

---

90 As an example, Henry Kissinger proposed six central questions for American strategy: What has to be prevented, if necessary alone?; What should we seek to achieve, if necessary alone?; What should we seek to achieve or prevent, if supported by an alliance?; What aims should not be pursued even if urged by Allies?; What is the nature of one's values?; and What applications depend in part on circumstance? The answers to the first two questions are reflected in the model as strategic ends and Minimum Level of Security, respectively, and the next two, pointing to the outer limits of a state's strategic aspirations as part of a global system and the limiting condition of its participation in the world order could easily be integrated, whereas the last two questions are more difficult to integrate. (The questions are developed for a 'responsible' US role 'in

including the strategic ends in the functions. These deficiencies are acknowledged and more work is needed to refine the model; however, it is a tool that enables a further analysis of the term defence.

3.3.2 Defence in the Strategical Analysis Model

Using the model introduced above, different understandings of defence can be described more precisely.

The traditional sequential and fixed connection between deterrence and defence in NATO thinking represents an understanding according to which the curve would be influenced by deterrence (and dialogue), and be kept above the line indicating the level of minimum security. Should that line be crossed, i.e. should deterrence fail, defence would take place. This was basically the planning assumption of NATO in its first age, so if one were to depict NATO's first age in the Strategical Analysis model, the shape of NATO's curve in the strategic environment would indicate an approach more or less limited to preventing a conventional and nuclear Soviet threat.

The interpretation of defence in NATO's second age was much wider. The then German Minister of Defence Peter Struck declared: "[Germany's] security is being defended not only, but also, in the Hindu Kush" (Struck 2004), implying defensive action well above a level of minimum security. This could be expressed in two graphic shapes. One understanding would be that defence encompasses all means employed to stop a curve from declining (= make sure the derivative remains positive). This considerably widens the scope of the term defence and either disregards other ways to achieve an upward movement, such as cooperation, nudging or rewards, or subsumes them under defence, considerably blurring the limitations of the term. Naturally it needs to be recognised that today defence is more than trenches and walls.

the evolution of a twenty-first-century world order' in: Kissinger 2014: 372–373).

The other option would be to introduce an additional line above the level of minimum security and declare every action below as 'defence'. In this view again all actions would be subsumed under the term 'defence', but only in a limited spectrum. Still this interpretation would allow defence to take place before a state's minimum level of security has been undercut.

The flexibility in the Strategical Analysis model can help overcome the dilemma of either choosing a black-and-white approach or a 'grey' one that simply makes use of every available means to prevent the curve from declining below the minimum level of security.

The model can display different strategic issues with different minimum levels of security for the respective functions. The relevant strategic issues, which mostly consist of threats or challenges in the case of a defence or military strategy, can have their own threshold of defence. And the flexible definition of the minimum level of security allows this to restrictively limit the breadth of the term 'defence':

Defence can only take place below the minimum level of security, but this minimum level of security can vary.

This is illustrated by figure 6 where three examples of security issues for an imaginative state or alliance are depicted.

The state's or alliance's population is very sensitive about a terrorist threat, thus the minimum level of security for the terrorism function is relatively high. Amongst other efforts, defence takes place most of the time—maybe also in the Hindu Kush—to achieve an acceptable level of security.

A certain vulnerability in the cyber realm could be acceptable, but in the example the threat level is constantly so high that the amount of security achieved is insufficient. Therefore the state or alliance will persistently undertake cyber defence measures.

At a specific moment relations to a peer state actor have deteriorated significantly, resulting in a very low level of security. However, this threat is, or has to be, accepted by the state or alliance without actively defending against the peer-state actor. If, however, the level of security has fallen below such a low minimum level as marked by

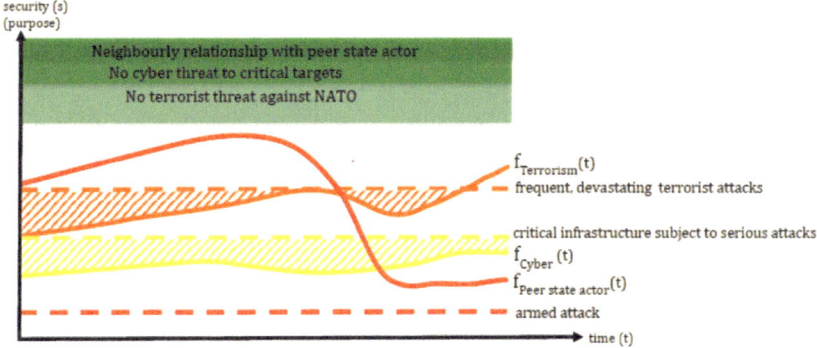

Fig. 6: Three examples of security functions with respective minimum levels of security. The shaded areas indicate where defence takes place.

armed attack, the state or alliance will likely have to concentrate all available means to defend against that threat.

This leads to another conclusion that can be drawn from the model. While the security level remains relatively high, defence can be a choice; defence would be the continuation of strategy with other means[91], just as Clausewitz has described the function of war in politics. A threshold of minimum security crossed at a very low level would lead to 'defence by necessity', in a way marking the end of strategy, just as Clausewitz's 'ideal' war indeed marks the end of politics.

So while the narrow description of defence as only taking place below the minimum level of security appears to be taken from the first age of NATO, it can still cover the more complex environment and also support the notion of NATO defending more actively as was suggested in its second age. Very likely NATO will have to defend every day, but still not everything NATO does in every respect is defence.

---

91 It is likely a failure of the higher-level strategy though, i.e. if a military strategy has to devise active, not just potential defence against a threat, the grand strategy or defence strategy has failed to maintain the minimum level of security.

The model even allows for the active air defence system mentioned earlier to defend (against a rogue terrorist) and deter (against a peer state actor) at the same time.

The model also shows the complex tasks for the strategist: the issues have to be clearly identified, the respective limits of minimum security defined, and then the approaches that together form the strategy have to be conceived. Given the interdependencies of the variables, and also the volatility and complexity of strategic environments, a strategy will not be able to formulate every function of every issue. The respective strategy will have to describe the variables, provide a frame to tailor the actions of a given state or alliance fitting to the task at hand and scale the required level of defence according to the respective threat to the security of the state or alliance.

4 Defence Today

Now that a historical and a theoretical view on defence have been presented, this chapter will examine the shape of defence today. In that respect the last five to six years are understood as part of the current phase of international relations. This phase and with it the third age of NATO began in the watershed year of 2014 with the Russian intervention in Crimea, the crisis in Ukraine, the Islamic State of Iraq and the Levant/and Syria (ISIL/ISIS) emerging as a state-like actor, and NATO's intervention in Libya. These events and other developments have led to a complex threat scenario for NATO (Sloan 2016: 318). Naturally, hybrid tactics are traditionally part of warfare and, as one of the key principles of strategy, all available means are employed and orchestrated (Major/Mölling 2015: 1–2). Consequently it should not come as a surprise when a state or an alliance is today faced with a multitude of challenges. However, the change in the strategic environment that took place in 2014 was unprecedented and goes well beyond a widened scope of the adversaries' means.

This leads to three points to be analysed: with regard to the strategic environment the first part of this chapter will discuss the behaviour of state actors and the variety of and interdependencies between other factors. The second part will then address the final aspect of NATO's recent development in its third age, which began in 2014.

4.1 Key Features of the Current Strategic Environment

The first age of NATO was characterised by an international order that was based on a balance of power. This system was replaced in the second age by an international order based on rules and an American hegemony. In the third age both, the respect for rules and the American ability to shape global politics, have declined drastically. This change in the international architecture affects all major actors, regardless of whether they promote the departure from the traditional order, seek to take advantage of the opportunities arising from changing patterns, or favour a status quo. The resulting considerations for an understanding of defence will be briefly presented in the following section. Subsequently, the multitude of other factors such as technological developments or globalisation, that not only influence each other but also the actors in the international arena, and consequently the interpretation of defence, will be discussed.

4.1.1 Behaviour of State Actors

Regardless of whether one's point of view is inclined towards realism, pacifism, or democratic peace theory, the most prominent actors in the international arena remain nation states. And while after the end of the Cold War multilateralism and international organisations were en vogue, current political tendencies favour unilateral action, strong states, and patriotism.[92] This leads to significantly more competitive and confrontational foreign policies resulting in attempts to enlarge national territories, proxy wars, trade and migration disputes, and a general abundance of conflict endangering or diminishing the security of nations. The protagonists are traditional or newly aspiring global actors or nations seeking regional dominance.

In the US, Barack Obama's internationalist agenda had been characterised by a clearly marked 'pivot to the pacific'; the Trump administration now has vocally promoted an 'America first' policy. NATO has been proclaimed 'obsolete and expensive' and a remnant from 'a long time ago' (Sayle 2019: 247). The world is perceived to be an arena of competition where self-interest and power will maximise a nation's security.

For President Trump this has been a continuum throughout history (Trump 2019), and his administration's foreign policy is a combination of isolationism, marked by limited active engagement in conflict regions or with a view to development aims, on the one hand and the attempt of containment through military strength and presence,

---

92 See very pointedly: Trump 2019: "The future does not belong to globalists. The future belongs to patriots."

sanctions, and the indirect support of partners such as Saudi Arabia on the other.

Protection is not sought from rules or international organisations, but has to be provided through bilateral agreements or one's own superiority. NATO and the UN are assessed on the basis of their utility to national interests and seen more as a burden than as an opportunity to provide security. For the UN this results in problems of effectiveness with regards to measures such as the Paris Climate arrangements and in practical problems stemming from pressure to 'achieve more with less' and decreasing financial contributions. For NATO even a spectre of doubt concerning the US commitment to the Alliance results in visible cracks in its cohesion and deterrence posture. The US dominance in military technology, numbers, and intelligence capability within NATO makes a conventional defence of the Euro-Atlantic area, but also an effective defence against unconventional threats, without American support unthinkable.

Russia undoubtedly seeks to increase its global influence and reclaim a more prominent role in international relations (Hartmann 2017: 310–312). It deliberately exploits opportunities to create situations that cannot be discussed without Russia at the table and succeeds in being treated at eye-level with the US despite of its mediocre economy and abundant domestic problems.[93]

Its military capabilities and operational advantage arising from a centralised, rigid organisational structure amount to a threat potential that should be taken seriously. Russia openly disregards international treaties and violates other nations' sovereignty with more or less covert activities and information operations as in the interventions in Ukraine.[94] Remarkably, Russia does not even abstain from adverse activities against NATO Allies.

---

93 See for example Russia's involvement in Syria and Ukraine (Erler 2017: 16).
94 In Ukraine particularly the annexation of Crimea and the support to separationists in eastern Ukraine; other Russian activities include covert

However, while Russia does target the cohesion of the Alliance and seeks to weaken its capacity to act, these actions very likely are not part of a large scheme to defeat NATO militarily in World War III. With indications of autocratic tendencies building up during his first tenure (Sloan 2016: 232), President Putin's policy changed dramatically after the 2011–2012 protests that began in the aftermath of his re-election as president. Before, the Russian people had remained calm as long as the economy improved, but then strength and autocracy were deemed necessary for the president to cling to power (Erler 2017: 21–22). Putin, utilising the proven tale of Russia as a suffering victim that is denied its proper role in the world (Sloan 2016: 310–311), could not trust a socialist party structure that had held together the USSR for decades, but had to rely on his personal networks. And while Putin's planning efforts usually follow elaborated strategic principles,[95] his decisions could be read as his interpretation of Machiavelli's 'Il Principe', but not necessarily as part of long-term strategic planning in the Chinese tradition.

China does have, and meticulously follows, a long-term regional and global strategy. It seeks to satisfy its need for resources, fos-

---

operations such as in Salisbury in 2018 or the assassination of Zelimkhan Khangoshvili in Berlin in August 2019; information operations through media outlets, or social media manipulation.

95   Hartmann 2017: 114–115, although relying heavily on an analysis by Stephen Covington, a vocal proponent of ,hawkish' interpretations. Covington provides knowledgeable background information on historical Russian thinking and an explanation of the mechanics of Russian strategy. However, his contradicting descriptions of Russia desiring to avoid war and at the same time posing a direct military threat (Covington 2016), and former predictions that were off the mark (such as his 2015 estimate of Russia trying to prevent a frozen conflict in Ukraine (Covington 2015: 9–10), make his conclusions for a current Russian strategy questionable, particularly when he ventures from the explanation of Russian mechanics to a presumed intent. Covington is Special Advisor for Strategic and International Affairs to NATO's Supreme Allied Commander Europe (SACEUR).

ter westward trading routes for the development of its problematic western regions, and strives for regional control and global influence as part of a multipolar world order (Erler 2017: 13–14). Traditional Chinese views on values and a perfected Chinese societal model, serving as a cultural example to the world, are complemented by Western approaches to technology and projection of influence. This course of action challenges the world order based on Western principles and a Western understanding of democracy (Kissinger 2014: 363–364). To advance its goals China primarily relies on economic and diplomatic instruments of power,[96] but the Chinese military is growing quickly in terms of size and capabilities. Currently it is able to project power on a regional scale, but soon interests and military activities could increasingly overlap with NATO's area of interest.

Influential European states such as France, Germany, and Great Britain have benefited greatly from a stable rules-based international order. Currently, however, they are internally suffering from the consequences of their liberal democracies: they are weakened by populist political movements and an increasing fragmentation of their populations. Externally, they are threatened by the harsh competition going on between nation states.

Individually, neither of them could keep up with larger actors such as the US or China, neither at the political or economic level nor in the military domain. Their hope rests in a resistant rules-based international order, strong institutions that remain based on democratic values and standards, and close cooperation in all areas, including defence. The next-best option could be bandwagoning with one of the major actors—after the "Brexit" Great Britain seems to at-

---

96 For example, it puts pressure on other states not to recognise Taiwan as a sovereign nation and pushes for own personnel to obtain influential positions in international organisations. China could recently claim leadership positions in the UN Development Program and the UN Food and Agriculture Organization, as well as the position of UN Special Envoy for the Great Lakes Region, exploiting the void of American influence.

tempt a combination of both, leaning towards the US and increasing its efforts to strengthen the UN at the same time.

Regional actors such as Iran and the Democratic People's Republic of Korea (North Korea) exploit the void left by the diminishing importance of a rules-based international order and the loss of tangible influence of the US. For North Korea a strong defensive posture, including a credible nuclear deterrent, has clearly led to increased international recognition and relative security from outside threats. This might set an example for other regional actors seeking more influence and protection for their regimes. A more aggressive Iranian stance and possible future nuclear capabilities could directly influence NATO's defensive posture, including for example a re-evaluation of the desired capabilities of NATO's Ballistic Missile Defence.

4.1.2 Variety of and Interdependencies Between Other Factors

To a large extent the behaviour of the actors mentioned above is a result of technological developments. These developments comprise inventions that open new dimensions in capability and pose previously unknown challenges to existing systems. Examples are new batteries or levels of automation that enable the production and use of extremely capable unmanned aerial systems. The next step could be quantum computing rendering a large part of the current encryption methods useless and possibly allowing for a wider exploitation of big data. The current trends in development clearly favour the offence. Increasing speed and flexibility, including the dual-use of systems, can deliberately or accidentally blur the intentions of an actor.[97]

Technological development also includes innovation. The diffusion of and access to modern technology shapes not only the character of high-tech societies and armies, but changes the whole of the strategic environment. Capable, high-tech off-the-shelf drones and other dual-use devices and reliable internet services including so-

---

97   A Russian example would be the development of the SSC-8 and SSC-X-9 missiles.

cial media are available in every corner of the world. Proliferation of sophisticated weapons and, in the worst case, of weapons of mass destruction is the other side of the coin of global technological development (Gerstein 2005: 36).

The increased technological capabilities of all actors are a catalyst in a highly reactive strategic environment.

Globalisation with all its positive effects also leads to vulnerabilities of states, requiring discussions and decisions regarding the level to which defence should extend. The German discussion was already mentioned, but again and again all nations see themselves confronted with challenges that emerge far away from their borders, but still have an impact on important security interests such as energy security or trade routes. Western states rely on security in far away regions such as the Persion Gulf or the Strait of Malacca and a virus spreading from the Far East can stun European societies and kill thousands on the other side of the globe.

To some extent, globalisation and technological developments lessen the importance of geography. Distance to a conflict does not even protect from direct harm any more. An increasing arsenal of long-range or geographically unrestricted means and shortened reaction times increase security risks and the cost of preventive measures.[98] This is not a new development,[99] but with the use of the cyber and space domains, automation, supersonic missiles and other assets, the end of the trend might be approaching, leading to a strategic environment where a multitude of actors can strike any target on the planet with a variety of means and virtually no preparation time.

However, geography retains its importance in a different respect. Human beings will always live in geographically defined areas and it

---

98 For the German situation see: Ehrhart/Neuneck 2016: 5.
99 In 1957 John Herz marked the use of gunpowder as the beginning of this trend. (Quoted from: Buhaug/Gleditsch 2006: 7. Buhaug and Gleditsch offer an analysis of the relationship between the proximity of actors and the likelihood of conflict).

has been pointed out that the ideological aspect of geography is not to be underestimated. Proximity to instability is a feature of the strategic environment for NATO. Different internal and external developments have led to a belt of instability around the North Atlantic Area, ranging from war-torn Ukraine and Syria to the increasing confrontation around Israel and a North African row of states that have yet to regain stability after the Arab Spring.[100] This belt provides a fertile breeding ground for other sources of instability and risks to security, such as terrorism and migration.

Internal instability and conflict are reflected in the foreign policies of many actors, both inside and outside of NATO. States and international organisations like the EU or NATO struggle to maintain their influence on the external environment; their behaviour is often driven by internal political needs and fragmentation, also offering opportunities for exploitation by other actors (Sloan 2016: 318–326), and thus bound to be less predictable. This can lead to conscious aggression or unintentional misunderstandings. While these factors make defence increasingly difficult and could suggest the need for traditional deterrence, the lack of predictability is highly problematic. If deterrence is faith, it requires trust in a potential adversary's behaviour. In order to be able to foresee or calculate that behaviour, influencing factors must be visible and the actors must resemble homines oeconomici who act reasonably for the objective benefit of their nation or cause. Over several decades a fairly stable consensus on red lines had been maintained, but in the current phase of history

---

100 Another expression used is 'Arc of Instability'. Joe Burton defines the Arc to range from the Sahel to Afghanistan and separates it from the eastern strategic direction, in particular Ukraine, calling one section 'static instability' and the other 'dynamic instability'. (Burton 2018: 153, 166–167.) However, this division appears artificial and is contradicted by Burton's further analysis of parallels. Also, more importantly, it does not take into account the role of actors, here predominantly Russia, as instigators and beneficiaries or exploiters of instability. Actors and instability are highly interrelated and cannot be separated geographically.

many a line has been crossed and confidence in the traditional world order or security mechanisms has been betrayed.

4.2 The Third Age of NATO

The third age of NATO resembles the sum of the first and the second age. NATO must provide collective defence and at the same time manage crises and promote stability beyond its borders (Stoltenberg 2016). The complex strategic environment and the fast pace of change increase the challenge for the Alliance to find solutions for a wide array of problems. Not all of these factors are new of course; in 1987 Eberhard Blum brought up the question: How can we improve our conventional defence in the face of financial constraints and dwindling populations? He then demanded conceptual solutions in the field of military politics, on both the operational-tactical and technological level (Blum 1987: 258).

After the end of the Cold War it was the military side of NATO that took the initiative to adjust the Alliance's strategic foundation to the new environment, [101] and again in the third age of NATO, the political level has shown no desire to review the in some aspects dated Strategic Concept of 2010. However, with its wide scope and formulations the Strategic Concept left enough room for summit declarations and lower-level work to change the course of the Alliance.

Since the Wales Summit in September 2014, there has been a paradigm change in the Alliance and with the adaptations that have taken place since then, the Alliance has shown some agility and solidarity (Broeks 2019: 4).

Taking the 2010 Strategic Concept plus the Wales, Warsaw and Brussels Summits as well as the Alliance's assurance and adaptation

---

101 In April 1990 the Military Committee was the first to be ready to "slaughter the sacred cow" MC 14/3 and gave the recommendation to undertake a detailed review of NATO's military strategy to the Secretary General and the Defence Ministerial in spring (Wittmann 2001: 221).

measures as a basis, the Military Committee has developed a new NATO Military Strategy, shifting from a reactive to a proactive approach. The new NATO Military Strategy was approved and signed by the Alliance's Chiefs of Defence in May 2019 and is the capstone document for the wider military adaptation and modernisation efforts. Retaining and complementing NATO's policy on Deterrence and Defence, Projecting Stability, and Fighting Terrorism, the NATO Military Strategy supports the Alliance's three core tasks and overarching messaging in the face of increasingly complex security challenges (Broeks 2019: 4).

The new Military Strategy can be regarded as the first such document since the 1968 MC 14/3 and will have further impact through its application within NATO's military instrument of power, the commitment of the Chiefs of Defence, and the strategy's influence on the decision making at the political level. The strategy will have to find responses to the main features of the strategic environment and how they impact the Alliance, however, the document is classified and not publicly available and thus its focus, details and take on defence cannot be analysed here.

For the defence of NATO, geography remains a decisive limiting factor.

In parts, NATO is today faced with the same problem that defined the early days of the Alliance: conventional defence of the easternmost Allies was virtually impossible then, and Europe's geography and the Alliance's disposition favoured a mobile defence offering space for time (Thoß 2006: 28). Geography hasn't changed, and the fact that NATO's eastern limits form a fragmented, overstretched outer line has made military defence anything but easier. However, the Baltic States are certainly not more exposed today than West-Berlin was in the Cold War (Sayle 2019: 246).

The geographic advantage of NATO remains its strategic depth, with enormous industrial capacities and resources and the relative security of the American continent. However, these advantages will come to bear only in long wars, making them less valuable for Allies that could potentially be overrun in a conflict and maybe only freed after a long and destructive struggle on their soil. In this respect, to-day's state of affairs still resembles the situation in the early years of the Cold War, and once again, NATO will have to find ways to leverage an increased strategic flexibility to cope with this dilemma.

It is generally accepted that the complex strategic environment threatens the security of NATO. However, threat perceptions differ greatly among the Allies, particularly regarding Russia (Sloan 2016: 307–308). The EU has started the endeavour of developing a common threat description and will find this difficult enough; for NATO such an enterprise would be even more challenging.

The eastern Allies sharing a border with Russia or looking back at a past of gruesome Soviet occupation tend to be very sensitive to the aggressive posture adopted by Russia. All of Europe was con-cerned about Russian actions in Ukraine, but Eastern Europe felt di-rectly threatened (Major/Mölling 2015: 2–3).Europeans living in the West or South of the continent are more directly affected by prob-lems other than the Russian posture, a view that could change given the increasing Russian presence in the Mediterranean and ongoing technological developments as even the Iberian Peninsula is getting within reach of land-based, dual-capable Russian intermediate range missiles. The Northern Allies still have a decent working relationship with Russia concerning the Arctic and also have to take into account the Swedish and Finnish political situation.

For Mediterranean Allies stability in the Sahel is an urgent con-cern that must be addressed in order to contribute to the prevention of migration, a topic also very important to Greece and Turkey. Turkey is the only NATO member bordering on Syria and directly faced with spill-over effects. They demand protection of their airspace and bor-der regions from accidental or purposeful infractions and help in the fight against terrorism. The question of what constitutes terrorism and what NATO's role in defending against it should be, also remains a point of heated discussion within the Alliance. On the other side of the spectrum, NATO as an organisation struggles to find a com-mon position on China that addresses the challenges, but also rec-ognises the opportunities of cooperation and dependencies. Another field for necessary adoption was exposed by the COVID-19-pandemic. Even with pandemics on most Allies' threat radar, preparations had remained abstract and the ongoing crisis will offer plenty lessons to learn from, but it will also leave national budgets severely strained.

Adding to these complex issues, two major subjects mostly pushed by the US strain the cohesion of the Alliance. One, outside of the scope of this paper, is the matter of appropriate burden sharing. The other question under discussion pertains directly to the interpretation of the defensive role of NATO. One position is in favour of NATO becoming more active, particularly with a view to entering a competition with Russia and/or possibly China, whereas other Allies would prefer NATO to play a strictly reactive role. This discussion will be continued in the final chapter of this paper.

In view of the multitude of diverging interests, and the contempt and disappointment about the Alliance that is sometimes openly displayed, one question begs to be answered: "Why does NATO still exist?"

In his recent book "Enduring Alliance", the Canadian historian Timothy Sayle very elegantly points out a convincing root cause for NATO's lasting existence:

> Allied leaders on both sides of the Atlantic viewed NATO as the issue of primary importance in both their transatlantic and even global affairs. NATO and the Pax Atlantica, the allies believed, provided the stability and peace that allowed for myriad other complicated non-security relationships between and among NATO allies, and also allowed for the allies to engage with the broader world. When, on occasion, allied leaders had to choose between preserving the Pax Atlantica or pursuing other national interests, they chose NATO. That is why NATO endures. (Sayle 2019: 9)

This conclusion could cause some concern and the line of thought will be picked up in the final chapter of this study.

5 Conclusion

This paper set out to deal with different aspects of the term defence. Chapters 2 and 3 elaborated on the different historical and theoretical aspects of what defence can be, how it can be described and analysed and what should not be called defence. Looking at the three ages of NATO, the respective understanding of defence and points of friction were laid out. The strategical analysis and the features and interdependencies characterising the current strategic environment built the case for a 24/7 defence in NATO, but without blurring the term and stretching it beyond reasonable limits. A flexible defence that is scalable to different threats could achieve this. What remains to be discussed is how NATO currently understands—and should understand—defence, and what this could mean for the Alliance's role in the world.

This concluding chapter will first summarise a few of the conclusions drawn in the above chapters on the historical perspective and the theories of and approaches to defence. Then some normative thoughts on NATO's current take on defence will be developed before in the final part of this chapter a short outlook will be presented both in terms of NATO's future as well as with regard to further scientific work.

5.1 Conclusions from History

The different historical examples illustrated in this paper showed very different approaches to defence that varied in scope, in the point in time when defence was put into action, and in the methods employed. The actors described all found themselves in a difficult strategic situation, where the state was at risk and the need to defend palpable.

Von Seeckt—under the impression of the restrictions imposed on Germany following the Versailles treaty—justified the need for armament with the size of his country, its exposed geographic position and its entanglement with events in the world (Seeckt 1930: 29).

NATO today spans the larger part of the European continent; it is geographically exposed at the fringes, with soldiers operating under the NATO flag far outside the Alliance's territory, straits to be controlled and long lines of communication to be protected. Technology and globalisation in general are leading to unprecedented entanglement in the world. Taking von Seeckt's perspective, one must conclude that NATO is in need of defence.

The notion of what exactly had to be defended differed from the very survival of a nation as in the Six-Day War, to the idea of a free world in the Truman Doctrine. Lambert adds a few more interesting purposes for defence, such as protecting the lives of a nation's citizens, an orderly way of life, soldiers on operation, or public goods and national treasures.[102] Other things worth defending could be values, a nation's freedom,[103] very broadly its interests, and also allies in a collective defence scenario.

Throughout NATO's history the terms deterrence and defence have been almost indivisible. The basic understanding was—and for some Allies still is—that defence (only) takes place if deterrence fails. At the same time, envisaging that the ultimate, nuclear deterrence might fail is not an option either, just as the reintegration of the employment of nuclear weapons in defensive planning as in the early days of NATO would hardly be acceptable to Allies today.

Containment thinking, or in modern terms 'competing', was reflected in the composition of the founding Allies: the decision was taken to expand the European side of NATO beyond the group of nations of the Brussels Treaty. But what was the designed destiny of NATO? There were no hints of a Hamiltonian view to be found, seeing the Alliance as the seed of a world order bringing down communism and securing global control for the West. The Treaty's references to

---

102 Lambert 2002: 44–47: "l'existence de la nation, la survie des citoyens, la vie civile courante, la vie des militaires en opex, biens collectifs et richesses nationales".

103 Including protection from blackmailing (Sayle 2019: 241–242).

the UN Charter point rather to a Jeffersonian approach. NATO was to follow and foster the global rules, grow strong from within and be an example of stability and values. This was again reflected after the end of the Cold War. There were no NATO victory celebrations and the Alliance did not actively expand or acquire, let alone occupy, new territory. During the Cold War and after, NATO remained open to nations that wanted to join, and the Alliance could rely on the attractiveness of membership being sufficient to draw applications.

What has changed considerably over time is how war is perceived, felt and influenced by the nations' societies and militaries. One extreme was seeing the strength and vigour of the population as one of the decisive factors in military campaigns. The other extreme was war being unthinkable for civilians to actually occur ever again, and in between these two lies the population's current role of spectators who follow wars in news shows. For a soldier patrolling the inner German border in the 1980s, nothing was more remote than the thought of actually fighting in a war. Today the vast majority of Bundeswehr soldiers has served in or supported operations, and the heavy losses in combat in Afghanistan and the 2009 bombing in Kunduz demonstrated to all Germans that there was indeed a war going on and that Germany was actively involved in it. Media coverage brings Syria, Iraq, or Mali to our TV screens every night—with Western soldiers involved in local conflicts, usually as the 'good guys' trying to bring peace and stability and always vastly superior in technology and firepower. As mentioned earlier, for societies, but also for many military thinkers and decision makers defence is no longer equal to the avoidance of war; instead victory in battle is becoming an indicator for successful defence and security.

However, a war with a peer state competitor, and particularly one with an impressive nuclear arsenal, would be something quite different. In such a war, there would be no victory; in the worst case it could end in complete nuclear devastation.[104]

The thinking of the second age of NATO must not be transferred to the challenge of a more assertive Russia. The Alliance does not have to prepare to win this war; NATO must prevent this war from taking place.

The adaptation of NATO will take some time. The political decision-making is still underway, and the Western societies have many pressing issues to discuss and agree upon. Particularly the European Allies will need some time and patience. After 9/11 they engaged in the fight against terrorism without being prepared—neither did they have the necessary equipment nor were their societies aware of what they were stepping into. Then, just as they had shifted their focus to out-of-area operations and their armies had switched from main battle tanks to IED-proof, lighter vehicles, the events of 2014 changed everything. Again unexpectedly—and still in the aftermath of a severe financial crisis –planning had to return to collective defence. This development and the strains of the COVID-19 pandemic will without doubt be reflected as an on-going dent in the security curve of the Strategical Analysis model and has to be addressed. However, putting too many burdens on already strained and diverging societies will have adverse effects on cohesion and decision-making and has to be prevented as well.

That is the golden thread running through NATO's history: the importance of cohesion and the US and the European Allies relying on each other. Blum was quoted earlier with a to-do list for the Alliance from 1987 that might as well have been drawn up for today's situation. He also identified the most important requirement for coping

---

104 Liddel Hart for example recognised that very early. Already in 1955 he denounced the idea of victory in a war with the Soviet Union as a fatal illusion (Hart 1955: 284).

with the problem set: The unity of the Alliance.[105] This remains true today: the unity of the Alliance must be clearly supported across all fields of NATO adaptation. It also provides an answer to the question how to minimize the risk of an adversary exploiting weaknesses of the Alliance. The reciprocal dependency will remain. In the face of an assertive Russia, the European Allies will continue to rely on a strong transatlantic bond and US safety guarantees. But the US also relies on its European Allies, even with an increasing focus on the Pacific, an endeavour that was begun cooperatively under Obama, and continued confrontationally under Trump. Seen from the Pacific, Europe is the strategic depth of the Alliance, as is the US seen from Russia. No NATO Ally can afford to lose either of them.

5.2 Conclusions from Theory

In the first part of the chapter on theories of and approaches to defence, several judicial views on defence were discussed. It was argued that the even though a conclusive definition of defence is difficult to identify, the scope of what is meant by 'defence' in international law is likely smaller than many nations perceive or claim it to be. Law evolves nationally with interpretations or political decisions, and internationally with nations acting, accepting the actions of others or developing conventions.

Legal considerations and adherence to accepted rules and interpretations provide legitimacy for all actions, including defensive ones. Domestically the careful and restrictive adaptation of rules to political realities supports social cohesion and leaves little vulnerability to be targeted.

In international relations, infractions of international law are not necessarily sanctioned juristically, but obvious, strong legitimacy

---

105 Blum 1987: 258: "The most important military-political imperative is the unity of the Alliance to the inside and out. It supersedes desirable and otherwise possible improvements of efficiency."

leads to international acceptance and support. Within an alliance this acceptance and support is expressed in cohesion. Actions of limited or doubtful legitimacy are likely to provoke differing views among allies, particularly in NATO as an explicitly democratic and norm-supportive organisation.

The considerations concerning deterrence in connection with the current strategic environment clearly point to the need for NATO to develop an adapted understanding of deterrence. There are concepts, including the perfect deterrence theory, that offer alternatives to classic deterrence.

(Nuclear) deterrence by punishment includes deterrence by the threat to do evil (Tucker 1985: 44–47). Regardless of questions of legitimacy or guilt, nuclear retaliation would equal a loss of humanity that is hardly thinkable or morally bearable, especially for countries whose societies are not accustomed to a life in the face of an existential threat. And a world in which the execution of this form of deterrence appears to be a valid option is hardly desirable either.

Deterrence by denial is evolving more and more into an active form of defence. This paper has shown that in the current strategic environment a continuous, scalable defence is required for NATO. Thus the Alliance has to free defence from the shackles of deterrence. Different functions of security affect the overall security of the Alliance and in some areas it may be necessary to actually defend even while deterrence continues in others.

NATO had identified resilience as its new 'first line of defence' even before COVID-19, but difficulties remain in implementing it as most issues lie within the exclusive political realm of the member states. At the Warsaw summit seven baseline requirements were defined for improved deterrence and protection.[106] Improved resilience and its value for the defence of the Alliance require NATO to clear-

---

106 The requirements encompass the continued delivery of governmental decision-making and services, provision of energy, water, and food, and maintaining of communications and traffic (Hartmann 2017: 110).

ly identify gaps—that have been exposed by COVID-19 in some, particularly health-related, areas—and desired strategic approaches. NATO must also increasingly involve its populations into its defence (Hartmann 2017: 121).

NATO needs mobile, flexible forces because of its geographic layout, its desire to project stability beyond its borders, and its obligation to be cost efficient. These forces can by their very nature appear offensive. Additionally, current technology, including long-range effectors, the ability to obscure the originator of an attack,[107] and dual-use capable assets, favours the offensive. According to Jervis, these two factors together lead to a doubly dangerous scenario, requiring careful posture management and clear communications to avoid unintended escalation.

The 'responsibility dilemma' that was introduced in the third chapter has to be taken into account when judging the contribution of Projecting Stability to the defence of the Alliance. Certainly a stable periphery positively influences the security of NATO, particularly with regard to threats to the Allies' territory. However, the responsibility dilemma can lead to other vulnerabilities and complex defensive situations outside of NATO territory. The associated benefits and risks have to be carefully balanced.

Attempts have been made at a certain kind of political warfare. As suggested by Hart, acts of civil disobedience, like those carried out by protest groups such as Anonymous or 'Extinction Rebellion', and the on-going protests in Hong Kong could be considered as political warfare, although it is not being employed by a state and not to its full extent. However, these movements have so far only had a very limited impact. Naturally none of the above actions was performed by entire societies, but in the increasingly fractured societies of the

---

107 Even when about 25 rockets hit the Saudi Arabian oil installations in Abqaiq and Khurais on September 14th, 2019, the identification of the perpetrator by the US, France, Germany, and the UK relied on circumstantial evidence pointing to Iran as the 'only plausible explanation' (quoted from BBC 2019).

West it even appears unlikely that a complete social opposition could be formed against an illegitimate government.[108] Instigating such a potential opposition also bears the grave danger of undermining rules-based thinking and could further endanger democratic structures. It could also invite adversaries to misuse the concept through propaganda and influence operations.

A militarily defensive defence was proven to be largely incompatible with NATO's geographic layout and its requirements in forces in the third chapter of this paper.

Contesting is a systemic approach that differs from the traditional defensive thinking of NATO. Of course that does not make it automatically wrong or dangerous, but a major shift in Alliance mindset and policy certainly requires good arguments demonstrating in particular why the current situation differs so considerably from earlier phases and why this would lead to the necessity for NATO to compete. As was pointed out, the replacement of the peace-crisis-war spectrum with a simple competition continuum is not convincing. The measures and examples described in the concept mostly focus on state actors, in particular large state actors. This would reflect the situation in the first age of NATO, when the Alliance was faced with an adversary of comparable, and in some aspects clearly superior capabilities. In that time the US did compete on a global scale and, as was shown in this paper, NATO might have been at times a part of that US-USSR competition, but the Alliance did not compete itself. Today, the paramount importance of advanced technological capabilities marks one difference to the first age of NATO. In the technological realm, it is necessary for NATO to compete and maintain the edge over potential adversaries.[109] A battle space that has changed so profoundly that NA-

---

108 Even if it has to be conceded that Mahatma Gandhi succeeded in uniting the at least equally divided Indian society behind his peaceful quest for independence, those differences were hardly overcome, but rather manifested once the oppressor had been ousted.

109 The necessity to maintain a technological edge was already identified in MC 14/1, which required NATO "to develop the required military force,

TO's capabilities are rendered useless would endanger the Alliance's deterrence posture and its ability to defend.

In the second age of NATO contest was not discussed to oppose terrorist organisations. Only lately have attempts been made to construct a competition model for terrorism. Not surprisingly they appear artificial and try to include aspects that do not fit the model. Both the competition continuum and the notion of contesting do not address other challenges, particularly phenomena such as migration or pervasive instability that do not emanate from wilful adversarial behaviour alone.

In summary, there is no need to change the paradigm from the first age of NATO when it comes to addressing large state actors, the second age never required contesting and the competition model fails to address other important challenges in the complex strategic environment of the third age.

The introduction and employment of the Strategical Analysis model has enabled a differentiated view on defence further emphasizing the need to maintain a limited and concise understanding of defence. But at the same time it could be demonstrated that NATO does defend actively, only not in every respect and not against all threats at all times. With the model the interdependencies between the various actions and factors influencing different threats to security have become clearly visible. They require a balanced, scalable posture and employment of forces, and the art of the strategist.

bearing in mind the economic and manpower situation of each nation, and to achieve and maintain technical superiority in its weapons." (NATO 1952: Appendix 2.b.). The fine difference between an edge in warfighting and general military superiority is spelt out most explicitly in the 1989 Brussels Summit's 'The Alliance's comprehensive concept of arms control and disarmament': "From its inception the Alliance of Western democracies has been defensive in purpose. This will remain so. None of our weapons will ever be used except in self-defence. The Alliance does not seek military superiority nor will it ever do so." (NATO 1989: para. 19).

5.3 To Be, or Not to Be – Defence for NATO Today

Condensed into brief conclusions, the results of this study lead to a number of recommendations and observations for NATO's future policy and its understanding of defence.

The first clear recommendation has already been indicated in this paper before: NATO should not compete or contest, but retain its more defensive interpretation of defence.

This includes the requirement to accept some degree of risk and even a lower level of security with respect to certain threats as was demonstrated in the Strategical Analysis model. This acceptance is something NATO has to re-learn.

The perception of vulnerability varies between Europe and America. For the US, since the Civil War, war has always taken place somewhere else. Generations of Americans considered their homeland absolutely safe from external threat, and war was a phenomenon perceived indirectly. This contributed to the impact of singular events such as Pearl Harbor and the 9/11 attacks. In Europe war and destruction devastated the continent twice in the course of the last century, and vulnerability has always been a constant consideration for all European states (Sloan 2016: 83–92).[110]

Today, the world, and particularly the US,[111] is used to limited wars of choice that are indeed the continuation of politics with oth-

---

110 Sloan 2016: 83–92.
111 This is very vividly described by Stephen Walt: "In Roosevelt's era, Americans were still reluctant to 'go abroad in search of monsters to destroy', but they fought with unexpected ferocity when attacked. They were slow to anger but united in response. The situation today is the exact opposite – they are quick on the trigger provided that none of them have to do very much once the bullets are flying. Instead of seeing war as a tragic necessity that is to be avoided if at all possible, Americans regard it as a rather sanitary "policy option" that takes place in countries most of them cannot locate and is conducted primarily by drones, aircraft, and volunteers." (Walt 2019).

er means. The Cold War, had it turned hot, would have been a total war, leading to what would have been the end of politics. Those are completely different concepts as has been pointed out by scholars discussing the 'two Clausewitzes'. NATO must not make the mistake of mixing them.

Even if the use of war has once again become more thinkable today and considerations on how to win wars have gained more weight, this thinking is dangerous with respect to threats posed by a peer state competitor. Here the emphasis must clearly remain on how to prevent war without risking unwanted escalation or misunderstandings. Contesting would increase this risk, rendering the possible strategic advantage that would come to bear if war broke out factually irrelevant. When two people fall off a cliff, it does not matter who hits the bottom first.

Additionally, contesting stresses and endangers cohesion within the Alliance on the military political and political level. The competition continuum and the approach of defending by contesting correspond to an American understanding of international relations. It is rather based on Hobbes' view of the world and thinking in terms of power and weakness. The European understanding of international relations rather resembles the Kantian approach that uses the categories of rules and institutions.[112]

The purpose of this paper is not to prove one of the concepts as superior to the other. However, the simple fact that fundamental differences in worldviews persist poses a threat to Alliance cohesion and requires consideration. It follows that finding a common denominator is essential. Although a more cautious approach might lead to the US feeling that NATO is not doing everything in its power, it would not put the foundation of the Alliance in question. A more assertive

---

112 The Hobbes/Kant image was designed by Robert Kagan (Varwick 2004: 205–206). It is certainly a simplification, in particular with a view to the more diverse European thinking with regard to a potential Russian threat, but still illustrates the fundamental difference in starting points of thinking.

approach, however, would jeopardize NATO's legitimation and its very acceptance in European societies.

NATO must find a balanced approach of demonstrating its ability to secure all Allies without provoking adversaries or alienating Allies.

For finding this necessary balance another central conclusion is important: as far as NATO is concerned, to be is to be safe.

Sayle's observation of how NATO members view the Alliance as a matter of primary importance and as the foundation for their respective foreign policy was introduced earlier. Sayle also quotes Bernard Montgomery who wrote that peace was in fact a by-product of military investment and preparedness, funnelled through NATO (Sayle 2019: 7). This view is in line with Joe Burton's analysis, which brings together the liberal and the realist explanations of NATO's endurance. The strength emanating from the joint political values, social and historical bonds and its institutional adaptation is complemented by NATO's role in power politics and its military capabilities (Burton 2018: 169–175).

Sharpening the point of these arguments and referring to the Alliance's history, one could claim that NATO's best defence is its very existence. It was not a specific action or operation against an adversary that was key to NATO's success. Kennan already pointed out in 1948 that the military cannot address the main danger of blackmail and 'political conquest', but he did not foresee that nevertheless a political and military alliance, that NATO would be key in prevailing over the decades to come (Sayle 2019: 13–14, 253).

With a view to the future, the conclusion and central claim therefore is: As long as NATO stands together, the Allies are safe.

If this thesis is accepted, two recommendations for further action can be deduced: 1. Cohesion must be maintained, and 2. The Alliance as a whole must remain strong enough to ensure its security.

Cohesion requires the Alliance to find a common language to address challenges and provide the minimum level of security for all Allies against all threats within the scope of a political and military alliance. NATO must also recognise cohesion as a value in itself and actively support and foster its unity. The most important aim must be to keep the division by the Atlantic as small as possible. An increasing division between Europe and the US could lead to strategic rivalry. This would in no way help tackling the security issues in the world (Varwick 2004: 225–226). The strength of the US is important for both the stability and the weight of NATO. Every US promise to NATO has a dividend in stability in Europe. European partners must contribute their share and, following their traditional approach to security, should also actively engage in supporting the rules-based international order, even outside of Europe. This does not have to be organized through NATO or unilaterally. The EU with its unique toolset could complement NATO's and the US's efforts to provide stability.

To guarantee sufficient strength of the Alliance as a whole, continued technological development and adaption are required, but that alone is not sufficient to safeguard against shifts in global power dynamics. Even if addressing some issues is outside of NATO's scope of influence, the Alliance nevertheless has to maintain a firm view on dependencies from resources, adaptation to climate change or other megatrends like shifts in population sizes and economic realities. It also must have sufficient buffer to cope with black swans.

These two lines of thought—1. do not contest, and 2. make sure you stay together and adapt—refute both the realist concept of security and the more Kantian approach, if applied individually. Neither will more accumulated power and relative advantage over potential adversaries increase NATO's security, nor will working towards a rules-based international order alone guarantee NATO's safety, as proven by the fading red lines of world order.

To stay in the Hamlet Soliloquy picture: determined action could mean the end of existence—and lead to an undiscovered country from whose bourn no traveller returns.[113] Consequently the safe advice would be: only to be, and not to sleep.

---

113 This is not only true with a view to Russia, but—keeping in mind historical examples and the responsibility dilemma—most visibly demonstrated in the ongoing struggle in Afghanistan after 9/11.

There are functions of security that can be positively influenced, including some that require defence. But as was illustrated in the description of the Strategical Analysis model, some variables influence more than one function. They have to be identified and very carefully adjusted. Within these limits, NATO can certainly protect its military advantage and guard against the danger of easy military defeat. It can support and demonstrate cohesion, but without building walls by using an 'us' and 'them' rhetoric. It can actively support the rules-based international order, but without unintended entanglement.

In particular, the adaption of NATO's defence has to include several aspects that were identified in this paper.

In the current strategic environment NATO needs a continuous, scalable defence. This does not mean that everything NATO does is defence, nor that the Alliance can deter or defend against all threats. With the realisation that some attackers cannot be deterred, the former thinking of 'deterrence and defence' has to be turned around: now it must be 'defence and deterrence'. NATO has to defend against attacks every day, but given that some attacks could be so devastating or that a defence against them would go beyond the thinkable scope, these attacks have to be deterred. A factually defensive posture and deterrence must still clearly demonstrate: NATO cannot be beaten cheaply! That is the effect required and the level of capability and scale NATO has to deliver.

This includes the example of the threat of a Russian attack on a Baltic Ally. NATO would very likely be unable to prevent operational defeat in defence with the resources the Alliance is willing to employ in preparation, the geographic realities, and the possible consequence of the force posture turning threatening. Consequently, defence can hardly be the right option—NATO will have to resort to deterrence. And it really is 'resort to', because for all the reasons explained above, a reliable defence would be preferable.

Defence with respect to some threats can take place without an invocation of Article 5 and still should be labelled accordingly: defence. Other actions, for example in the framework of Projecting Stability or the Fight against Terrorism should not be called defence, and most certainly not all actions should simply be called contesting.

Successful defence, and certainly also deterrence, require flexibility in response—regarding the available military options, but if possible across different instruments of power. In times of complex, hybrid threats the existing means of resilience, defence, and deterrence, have to be better connected and the mixture of civilian and military components appropriately adjusted (Major/Mölling 2015: 3–4).

The fact that a rules-based international order based on democratic principles cannot guarantee NATO's security on its own does not render it useless. Securing such an international order is the purpose of NATO. The existence of this order is the overall desired state (not the 'end'-state though, as history continues!), and also provides a fundamental value and a certain degree of security when intact. World orders break either when the concepts or foundations for their legitimacy shift (religion vs. different religion vs. secularism vs. racism...) or when the old order fails to accommodate a major change in power relations. The balancing of the two aspects of order is the essence of statesmanship (Kissinger 2014: 365–367). NATO faces the same challenge: To remain safe, it must m'l'he scope of this paper is far too limited to deal with these difficult questions, but they need to be discussed and answered, because they have repercussions for the security and the defence of the Alliance.aintain its power, but without jeopardising its accepted legitimacy and without damaging the order its legitimacy is based on.

5.4 Outlook

Edward Luttwak once warned that national strategies laid down in public statements and documents and any conclusions drawn from their analysis should be taken with a pinch of salt:

> National strategies, grand or not so grand must always be inferred from what is done or not done, and are never described in

documents—or not, at any rate, in documents that might see the light of day. Official documents that purport to present 'national strategies,' which are of course filled with fine sentiments and noble promises, are abundant, but what they contain is romance, not policy guidance or military directives meant in earnest. (Luttwak 2016: xi)

In this paper all of these sources—public statements and declarations, released internal documents, but also actions—have been sourced to paint the picture of defence. As this study is not only aimed at academic scholars, Luttwak's words should also remind decision makers not to only write and agree on sophisticated strategies, but also to employ them and adhere to them.

Hopefully NATO's Military Strategy includes more than 'fine sentiments and noble promises', but still it should be made available in a public version—not only for scholars, but also to provide the basis for an informed public debate. Currently statements to the public about this new military capstone document are largely limited to informed individuals citing certain aspects of the paper that appear to appeal to their target audiences,[114] without providing sufficient content and context to facilitate an objective discussion of the Alliance's direction of travel.

And yet, such a discussion would be desirable, because it could provide some guidance on the freedom of action of the Alliance, inform the ongoing political adaptation process and possibly spark interest in security matters. The lack of interest in world events is also part of the general disenchantment with politics and representation in Western democracies, but this is a matter the analysis of which would go beyond the scope of this paper.

---

114 Chairman of the Joint Chiefs of Staff, General Dunford for example limited the document to a "war strategy for Russia" (Muñoz 2019), which paints quite a different picture than Broeks does (Broeks 2019: 4).

Following the central claim of this study and assuming that NATO despite all challenges still stands and defends together, currently NATO itself is safe.

Still, questions remain: how to project stability, how to do cooperative security? And even with regard to 'defence', not all details are clear. For example, it remains to be decided how to protect the fringes, both geographically and regarding the term security itself. This study has provided some insights on how to deal with threats, but even if a flexible and persistent defence and deterrence is implemented, it will likely not prevent poison attacks and it will not help Ukraine.

Zones of different security, or the perception of such differences, within NATO damage the political, geographic and military unity of the Alliance (Blum 1987: 258). Clearly it is required to tailor the efforts of defence not only to the threats, but also to the needs and sentiments of the different Allies. In what way this can be achieved is a difficult question not only for day-to-day political decisions; in fact, it is a question of distributive justice: One possibility could be an equity of chance, meaning that NATO invests the same amount of resources and efforts into each Ally's security; another possibility would be an equity of result, seeking to provide the same level of security for each Ally. The latter approach might appear more desirable, but keeping in mind that NATO is less poised for some threats than others, it might overstretch expectations. It also implies that in NATO everyone has a common understanding of what has to be defended. Eventually, Allies will have to accept that NATO will not be able to do everything. Who seeks to defend everything, defends nothing.[115]

---

115 Admittedly, the original expression refers to a different context: Friedrich II. von Preußen (Friedrich der Große) (1748), Die Generalprinzipien des Krieges und ihre Anwendung auf die Taktik und Disziplin der Preußischen Truppen, Berlin, p. 14.

6 Bibliography

Afheldt, Horst (1984), Defensive Verteidigung – warum?, in: Weizsäcker, Carl Friedrich von (ed.), Praxis der defensiven Verteidigung (Friedensstrategien 1), Sponholtz: Hameln, p. 13–28.

Ameling, Walter (2011), The Rise of Carthage to 264 BC, in: Hoyos, Dexter (ed.), A Companion to the Punic Wars, Wiley & Blackwell: Chichester, p. 39–57.

Anderson, Sulome (2019), Hezbollah Readies for Next War Against Israel.

Anslover, Nicole (2014), Harry S. Truman. The Coming of the Cold War, Routledge: New York.

Apel, Hans (1979), Grundgesetz und Verteidigung, in: Information für die Truppe 11/79, p. 24–39.

ARD (2010), Tagesschau Extra, 31 May 2010, www.programm.ard.de/TV/Programm/Sender/?sendung=281065919080905, accessed on 15-09-2019.

BBC (2019), Iran Rejects Fresh Accusations Over Saudi Oil Attack, in: BBC.com, https://www.bbc.com/news/world-middle-east-49805591, accessed 02-10-2019.

Bleckmann, Bruno (2016), Der peloponnesische Krieg, C.H. Beck: Munich.

Blum, Eberhard (1987), Konventionelle Verteidigung: Ein Element der Abschreckung, in: Europäische Wehrkunde 5/87, p. 258–260.

Booth, Ken/Wheeler, Nicholas (1987), Beyond the Security Dilemma: Technology, Strategy and International Security, in: Jacobsen, Carl (ed.), The Uncertain Course. New Weapons, Strategies and Mind-Sets, Oxford University Press: Oxford, p. 313–338.

Bredow, Wilfried von (2014), Grenzen. Eine Geschichte des Zusammenlebens vom Limes bis Schengen, Theiss: Darmstadt

Brodie, Bernard (1946), The Absolute Weapon, Harcourt: New York.

Broeks, Jan (2019), The Necessary Adaptation of NATO's Military Instrument of Power (NATO Defence College (NDC) Policy Brief No. 14), Rome.

Brussels Treaty (March 17, 1948), quoted from www.nato.int/cps/en/natohq/official_texts_17072.htmhttps://www.nato.int/cps/en/natohq/official_texts_17072.htm, accessed 19-08-2019.

Buhaug, Halvard/Gleditsch, Nils Petter (2006), The Death of Distance? The Globalization of Armed Conflict, in: Kahler, Miles/Walter, Barbara F. (eds.), Territoriality and Conflict in an Era of Globalization, Cambridge University Press: New York, www.researchgate.net/publication/228685014_The_death_of_distance_The_globalization_of_armed_conflict/link/553161750cf27acb0dea9590/download, accessed 24-09-2019

Bülow, Christoph von (1984), Der Einsatz der Streitkräfte zur Verteidigung. Eine Untersuchung zu Artikel 87 a II GG, Peter Lang: Frankfurt a.M.

Burton, Joe (2018), NATO's durability in a Post-Cold War World, State University of New York Press: New York.

Clausewitz, Carl von (1832), Vom Kriege, Berlin, http://www.clausewitz.com/readings/VomKriege1832/TOC.htm, accessed on 14-07-20.

Clinton, Hillary (2011), America's Pacific Century. The Future of Politics Will Be Decided in Asia, Not Afghanistan or Iraq, and the United States Will Be Right at the Center of the Action, in: foreignpolicy.com, www.foreignpolicy.com/2011/10/11/americas-pacific-century, accessed 10-09-2019.

Comité Strategique (1996), Dossier d'information. Ministère de la defense, Paris.

Cook, Steven (2019), Israel Is Doing All the Dirty Work Against Iran. The United States Came Up With "Maximum Pressure" – but the Israeli Government is the Only One Carrying It Out, in: foreignpolicy.com, www.foreignpolicy.com/2019/09/04/israel-is-doing-all-the-dirty-work-against-iran, accessed on 05-09-2019.

Covington, Stephen (2015), Putin's Choice for Russia. Belfer Defense and Intelligence Projects, www.belfercenter.org/sites/default/files/files/publication/Putins%20Choice%20web%203.pdf, accessed on 28-09-2019.

Covington, Stephen (2016), The Culture of Strategic Thought Behind Russia's Modern Approaches to Warfare (Belfer Defense and Intelligence Projects), www.belfercenter.org/sites/default/files/files/publication/Culture%20of%20Strategic%20Thought%203.pdf, accessed on 29-09-2019.

Crabb, Cecil (1982), The Doctrines of American Foreign Policy. Their Meaning, Role, and Future, Lousiana State University Press: Baton Rouge/London.

Crawford, James (2019), Brownlie's Principles of Public International Law, Oxford University Press: Oxford.

de Maizière, Ulrich (1993), Die politische und ethische Legitimation der Verteidigung, in: Europäische Sicherheit 9, p. 462–463.

Despite a Pause in Hostilities, Militia Fighters and Experts Believe the Two Sides Could Stumble Into Their First All-Out Conflict Since 2006, in: foreignpolicy.com, www.foreignpolicy.com/2019/09/04/hezbollah-readies-for-new-war-against-israel-lebanon-drone-strikes/, accessed on 05-09-2019.

Deutscher Bundestag und Bundesarchiv (ed.) (1981), Der parlamentarische Rat 1948–49 (Akten und Protokolle 2), Der Verfassungskonvent auf Herrenchiemsee, Boppart am Rhein.

Dunn, Keith/Staudenmaier, William (eds.) (1985), Alternative Military Strategies for the Future. Westview Press: Boulder/London.

Ebert, Theodor (1981), Soziale Verteidigung. Historische Erfahrungen und Grundzüge ihrer Strategie, Westdeutscher Verlag: Waldkirch.

Ehrhart, Hans-Georg/Neuneck, Götz (2016) Sicherheitspolitische Bedrohungen und Risiken. Zivile Verteidigung und Zivilschutz aus der Sicht der Friedens- und Konfliktforschung, in: Bevölkerungsschutz 3/2016, p. 2–6.

Engelmann, Wolfgang (1978), Die Nordflanke der NATO: Bedeutung, Bedrohung und Verteidigung, in: Marine-Rundschau 3/1978, p. 137–149.

Erler, Gernot (2017), Im Machtdreieck von Putin, Xi Jinping und Trump. Die
neue Weltordnung 100 Jahre nach der Oktoberrevolution, Friedrich-
Ebert-Geächtnis-Vortrag 2017, Heidelberg, https://www.ebert-gedenksta-
ette.de/pb/site/Ebert-Gedenkstaette/get/params_E949348932_Dattach-
ment/1886158/Friedrich-Ebert-Ged%C3%A4chtnisvortrag_2019_web.pdf,
accessed on 15-07-2020.

Fattor, Eric (2014), American Empire and the Arsenal of Entertainment. Soft
Power and Cultural Weaponization, Palgrave Macmillan: New York.

Federal Constitutional Court (Bundesverfassungsgericht), Judgment of the
First Senate of 15 February 2006 - 1 BvR 357/05 -, paras. 1–156).

Friedrich II. von Preußen (Friedrich der Große) (1748), Die Generalprinzipien
des Krieges und ihre Anwendung auf die Taktik und Disziplin der Preußischen Truppen, Berlin.

Fukuyama, Francis (1992), The End of History and the Last Man, Free Press:
London/New York.

Gates, David (1991), Nonoffensive Defence: Alternative Strategy for N. A. T. O.,
New York.

German Criminal Code (Strafgesetzbuch), quoted from dejure.org, www.deju-
re.org/gesetze/StGB/32.html, accessed on 14-09-2019.

Gernet, Jaques et al. (1990), Die Große Mauer. Augsburg

Gerstein, Daniel (2005), Securing America's Future. National Strategy in the
Information Age, Praeger Publishers: Westport.

Giermann, Christian (1991), "Out-of-Area"-Einsatz von Seestreitkräften… ein
Stück Deutschland, in: Europäische Sicherheit 7/1991, p. 396.

Glaser, Charles (1997), The Security Dilemma Revisited, in: World Politics 50/1,
p. 171–201.

Goblirsch, Josef (1984), Neue Leitidee für die Verteidigung: Technotaktik, in:
Weizsäcker, Carl Friedrich von (ed.), Praxis der defensiven Verteidigung,
Sponholtz: Hameln, p. 121–135.

Gray, Colin (2010), The Strategy Bridge. Theory for Practice, Oxford University
Press: Oxford.

Grillo, Michael (2003), Harry S. Truman and the Legacy of Containment, in:
Gleek, Charles et al. (ed.), Presidential doctrines. National Security from
Woodrow Wilson to George W. Bush, Nova Publishers: New York, p. 41–58.

Grotius, Hugo (1625), De iure bellis ac pacis (The Law of War and Peace).

Hacke, Christian (2004), Die USA als globaler Akteur. Zu den transatlantischen
Beziehungen im Zeichen des Krieges gegen den Terror, in: Die politische
Meinung 49, p. 31–36.

Haglund, David (2002), Quelles fontières ,naturelles' pour l'OTAN?, in: La revue
internationale et stratégique 47 (3), p. 37–45.

Halbfinger, David et al. (2019), Israel Counters Iran in Flare-Up of Shadow War, in: The New York Times, 29-08-2019, Sec.A, p.1.

Hardy, James (2014), Strong Constitution. Japan Looks to Reset Its Policy on Self-Defence, in: Jane's Intelligence Review 26/6, p. 34–38.

Hart, Liddell (1955), Abschreckung oder Abwehr, Rheinische Verlags-Anstalt Wiesbaden (Originaltitel: Deterrent or Defense).

Hartmann, Uwe (2017), Resilienz als selbstkritische Verteidigungskonzeption von NATO und EU, in: Hartmann, Uwe/Rosen, Claus von (eds.), Jahrbuch Innere Führung. Die Wiederkehr der Verteidigung in Europa und die Zukunft der Bundeswehr, Berlin, p. 109–128.

Herz, John (1950), Idealist Internationalism and the Security Dilemma, in: World Politics 50 (2), p. 157–180.

Hoberg, Kai (2018), Abschreckung in Cyberspace. Strategische Überlegungen zur fünften Dimension der Kriegsführung (GIDS Analyis 2), Budrich Uni-Press: Berlin/Opladen/Toronto.

Hoyos, Dexter (2011), The Outbreak of War, in: Hoyos, Dexter (ed.), A Companion to the Punic Wars, Wiley & Blackwell: Chichester, p. 131–148.

Hunt, Michael (1987), Ideology and US Foreign Policy, Yale University Press: New Haven/London.

Huntington, Samuel (1984), Conventional Deterrence and Conventional Retaliation in Europe, in: International Security 8 (3), p. 32–56.

Interavia (1972), Abwehr der neuen Bedrohung – England plant eine flexible Verteidigung, in: Interavia. Internationale Revue für Luftfahrt, Raumfahrt und Elektronik 9, p. 960–963.

Ipsen, Knut (2009), Verteidigung: neue Dimension eines Völkerrechts- und Verfassungsbegriffs?, in: Sicherheit und Frieden 27, p. 266–274.

Ito, Narihiko (2006), Der Friedensartikel der Japanischen Verfassung. Für eine Welt ohne Krieg und Militär, Agenda Verlag: Münster.

Japanese Constitution (1947), The Prime Minister of Japan and His Cabinet, www.japan.kantei.go.jp/constitution_and_government_of_japan/constitution_e.html, accessed on 06-09-2019.

Jervis, Robert (1978), Cooperation Under the Security Dilemma, in: World Politics 30, p. 169.

Keller, Patrick (2012), Die Verteidigungsstrategie der USA und ihre Auswirkungen auf Europa, in: Der Mittler-Brief 27/2, p. 1–8.

Kissinger, Henry (2014), World Order, Penguin Press: New York.

Koliopoulos, Constantinos/Platias, Athanassios (1956), Thucydides on Strategy. Grand Strategies in the Peloponnesian War and Their Relevance Today, Oxford University Press: New York.

Komer, Robert (1983), Thinking About Strategy. A Practitioners Perspective, in: Dunn, Keith/Staudenmaier, William (ed.), Alternative Military strategies for the Future, Westview Press: Boulder/London, p. xi–xvii.

Kubina, Michael (2011), Die SED und ihre Mauer, in: Henke, Klaus-Dietmar (ed.), Die Mauer. Errichtung, Überwindung, Erinnerung, Deutscher Taschenbuchverlag: Munich, p. 83–95.

Kubina, Michael (2011), Die SED und ihre Mauer. Der Weg vom Penetrations- zum Fluchtverhinderungswall, in: Gedenkstätte Berliner Mauer (Berlin Wall Memorial), www.berliner-mauer-gedenkstaette.de/de/uploads/50jahrestag_tagung_dokumente/kubina-die-sed-und-ihre-mauer.pdf, accessed on 12-09-19.

Lambert, Denis (2002), Après le 11 septembre: dissuasion, défense active et défense passive, in: Défense Nationale 58 (5), p. 40–54.

Lamothe, Dan (2019), New Coast Guard Strategy for the Arctic Calls for 'Projecting Sovereignty' to Contest China and Russia, in: Washington Post, 22-04-2019, www.washingtonpost.com/national-security/2019/04/22/new-coast-guard-strategy-arctic-highlights-projecting-sovereignty-china-russia-look-north/, accessed on 09-09-2019.

Lovell, Julia (2006), The Great Wall. China Against the World 1000 BC – AD 2000, Grove Press: London.

Löwenstein, Stephan (2006), Jung: Wir müssen Verteidigung neu definieren, in: Frankfurter Allgemeine Zeitung, 02-05-2006, p. 1, 5.

Luhde, Thorsten/Tiede, Tanja (2003), Sicherheitspolitische Herausforderungen nach dem 11. September 2001. Aus britischen und französischen Fachzeitschriften (SWP Zeitschriftenschau 03/2003), SWP: Berlin.

Luttwak, Edward (2016), The Grand Strategy of the Roman Empire. From the First Century CE to Third, Johns Hopkins University Press: Baltimore.

Machiavelli, Niccolò (1531/1977): Discorsi. Gedanken über Politik und Staatsführung, A. Kröner: Stuttgart.

Magenheimer, Heinz (1986), Die Verteidigung Westeuropas. Doktrin, Kräftestand, Einsatzplanung – eine Bestandsaufnahme aus Sicht der NATO, Bernard & Graefe Verlag: Koblenz.

Major, Claudia/Mölling, Christian (2015), Eine hybride Sicherheitspolitik für Europa. Resilienz, Abschreckung und Verteidigung als Leitmotive (SWP-Aktuell 31), https://www.swp-berlin.org/fileadmin/contents/products/aktuell/2015A31_mjr_mlg.pdf, accessed on 15-07-2020.

Marston, Hunter (2019), The U.S.-China Cold War Is a Myth. The 20th Century's Great Standoff Doesn't Explain the Emerging Dynamic Between Washington and Beijing, in: foreignpolicy.com, 06-09-2019, https://foreignpolicy.com/2019/09/06/the-u-s-china-cold-war-is-a-myth/?utm_source=PostUp&utm_medium=email&utm_campaign=14854&utm_term=Editor, accessed 09-09-2019.

Mazarr, Michal (2018), Understanding Deterrence, in: RAND Perspectives, RAND Corporation, www.rand.org/content/dam/rand/pubs/perspectives/PE200/PE295/RAND_PE295.pdf, accessed on 15-09-2019.

McGhee, George (1990), The US-Turkish-NATO Middle East Connection, Palgrave Macmillan: London.

Militärgeschichtliches Forschungsamt (ed.) (1975), Verteidigung im Bündnis. Planung, Aufbau und Bewährung der Bundeswehr 1950–1972, Bernard & Graefe Verlag: Munich.

Moschek, Wolfgang (2010), Der Limes. Grenze des Imperium Romanum, Wissenschaftliche Buchgesellschaft: Darmstadt.

Munoz, Carlos (2019), NATO Tackles Growing Russia, China Threat with New Military Strategy, 30-30-30 plan, in: The Washington Times, 29-05-2019, www.washingtontimes.com/news/2019/may/29/joseph-dunford-nato-military-strategy-tackle-russi/, accessed on 18-08-2019.

Murray, Williamson (2013), Thucydides. Theorist of War, in: Naval War College Review 66 (4), p. 1–17.

North Atlantic Treaty Organization (1949), North Atlantic Treaty, NATO, www.nato.int/cps/en/natolive/official_texts_17120.htm, accessed on12-09-2019.

North Atlantic Treaty Organization (1989), The Alliance's Comprehensive Concept of Arms Control and Disarmament Adopted by the Heads of State and Government at the Meeting of the North Atlantic Council, Brussels, nato.int, https://www.nato.int/cps/en/natohq/official_texts_23553.htm?, accessed on 30-08-2019.

North Atlantic Treaty Organization (2018), Framework for Future Alliance Operations. 2018 report, NATO, www.act.nato.int/images/stories/media/doclibrary/180514_ffao18.pdf, accessed on 07-09-2018.

North Atlantic Treaty Organization, Military Commitee (1952), Military Decision MC 14/1, Paris.

North Atlantic Treaty Organization, Military Commitee (1968), Military Decision MC 14/3. Overall Strategic Concept for the Defense of the North Atlantic Treaty Organization Area, Brussels.

Rosenfeld, Stephen (1993), NATO's Last Chance, in: Washingtonpost.com, www.washingtonpost.com/archive/opinions/1993/07/02/natos-last-chance/22054ea7-5958-44b0-9e6a-212ee1da51de/, accessed on 11-09-2019.

Roth, Günter (1989), Clausewitz und die operative Idee bei Schlieffen und Manstein. Der Versuch einer vergleichenden Betrachtung des „Schlieffen- und Mansteinplanes als Frage der Durchgängigkeit Clausewitzscher Theorien im deutschen strategisch-operativen Denken und dessen Bedeutung für die Verteidigungsplanung der NATO, Potsdam.

Sayle, Timothy (2019), Enduring Alliance. A History of NATO and the Postwar Global Order, Cornell University Press: Ithaca/London.

Schallmayer, Egon (2006), Der Limes. Geschichte einer Grenze, C.H. Beck: Munich.

Schelling, Thomas (1966), Arms and Influence, Yale University Press: New Haven.

Schmid, Johann (2006), Der Präventivangriff. Gedanken zur Dialektik von Angriff und Verteidigung bei Carl von Clausewitz, untersucht am Beispiel des Sechstagekrieges von 1967, in: Österreichische Militärische Zeitschrift 44, p. 607–612.

Schmid, Johann (2011), Die Dialektik von Angriff und Verteidigung. Clausewitz und die stärkere Form des Kriegführens, Springer VS: Wiesbaden.

Schröder, Gerhard (1968): Ansprache des Bundesministers der Verteidigung, Dr. Gerhard Schröder, vor der Versammlung der Westeuropäischen Union am 17. Oktober 1968 in Paris, in: Information für die Truppe, Sonderbeilage 1969, Bonn.

Sebata, Takao (2007), Japan's Dilemma and a Problem of the Right to Collective Self-Defence Under the 1997 Guidelines, in: The Korean Journal of Defense Analysis 19 (3), p. 145–166.

Seeckt, Hans von (1930), Landesverteidigung, Verlag für Kulturpolitik: Berlin.

Shaw, Malcolm (82017), International Law, Cambridge University Press: Cambridge.

Sloan, Stanley (2016), Defense of the West. NATO, the European Union and the Transatlantic Bargain, Manchester University Press: Manchester

Speech at the Harvard Kennedy School, NATO, www.nato.int/cps/en/natohq/opinions_135317.htm, accessed on 14-08-2019.

Stoltenberg, Jens (2016), The Three Ages of NATO: An Evolving Alliance.

Struck, Peter (2004), Regierungserklärung des Bundesministers für Verteidigung zum neuen Kurs der Bundeswehr vor dem Deutschen Bundestag am 11. März 2004 in Berlin. Bulletin 23-1, Berlin.

Stupka, Andreas (2008), Strategie denken, Truppendienst: Vienna.

Supreme Court of Colorado (1964), The People of the State of Colorado, Plaintiff in Error, v. Charles E. la Voie, Defendant in Error. 395 P.2d 1001 (1964), quoted from Justia US Law, www.law.justia.com/cases/colorado/supreme-court/1964/20899.html, accessed on 15-09-2019.

Tang, Shiping (2009), The Security Dilemma: A Conceptual Analysis, in: Security Studies 18, p. 587–623.

The Crown Prosecution Service, Palmer v R, (1971) AC 814; Approved in R v McInnes, 55 Cr App R 551, www.cps.gov.uk/legal-guidance/self-defence-and-prevention-crime, accessed on 14-09-2019.

Thoß, Bruno (2006), NATO-Strategie und nationale Verteidigungsplanung. Planung und Aufbau der Bundeswehr unter den Bedingungen einer massiven atomaren Vereltungsstrategie 1952–1960, De Gruyter Oldenbourg: Munich.

Thucydides (translated by Warner, Rex (1972), History of the Peloponnesian War, Hammondsworth.

Tiedtke, Stephan (1986), Abschreckung und ihre Alternativen. Die sowjetische Sicht einer westlichen Debatte, Forschungsstätt der Evangelischen Studiengemeinschaft: Heidelberg.

Trombley Averill, Stephanie (2012), Truman and NATO, in: Margolies, Daniel (ed.), A Companion to Harry S. Truman, Wiley & Blackwell: Chichester, p. 410–427.

Truman, Harry (1947), President Truman's Message to Congress March 12, 1947, Document 171, 80th Congress, 1st Session, Records of the United States House of Representatives, National Archives.

Trump, Donald (2019), Remarks by President Trump to the 74th Session of the United Nations General Assembly, in: The White House, www.whitehouse.gov/briefings-statements/remarks-president-trump-74th-session-united-nations-general-assembly, accessed on 25-09-2019.

Tucker, Robert (1985), The Nuclear Debate. Deterrence and the Lapse of Faith, Holmes & Meier: New York.

United Nations Security Council (1990), Resolution 678 Iraq-Kuwait, New York, November 29, 1990, United Nations, www.unscr.com/en/resolutions/678, accessed 26-08-2019.

US Department of State (1957), American Foreign Policy 1950–1955, Basic Documents, Vol. I, 6446.

US Joint Chiefs of Staff (2019), Competition Continuum. Joint Doctrine Note 1-19, Washington.

Varwick, Johannes (2004), Die Nordatlantikorganisation und der amerikanische ‚War on Terrorism'. Transformation in die Bedeutungslosigkeit oder Neuanfang?, in: Pradetto, August (ed.), Sicherheit und Verteidigung nach dem 11. September 2001. Akteure – Strategien – Handlungsmuster (Strategische Kultur Europas 1), Peter Lang: Frankfurt a.M., p. 201–226.

Varwick, Johannes/Woyke, Wichard (2000), Die Zukunft der NATO. Transatlantische Sicherheit im Wandel, Springer VS: Wiesbaden.

Walt, Stephen (2019): There Once Was a President Who Hated War. American Elites Used to See War a Tragic Necessity, now They're Completely Addicted to It, in: foreignpolicy.com, foreignpolicy.com/2019/08/18/there-once-was-a-president-who-hated-war, accessed on 19-08-2019.

Walt, Steven (1987), The Origins of Alliances, Cornell University Press: New York.

Warner, Mark (2003), The Axis and the Empire, in: Gleek, Charles/Grillo, Michael/Watson, Robert P. (eds.), Presidential Doctrines. National Security from Woodrow Wilson to George W. Bush, Nova Science Publishers: New York, p. 95–111.

Weinheimer, Hans-Peter (2006), Asymmetrische Kriegführung und nationale Sicherheitsvorsorge. Eine Begründung für die erforderliche Anpassung des Systems „Innere Sicherheit" in Deutschland an die neuen Risiken und Gefahren, in: Der Mittler-Brief 4/2006, p. 1–8.

Wirtz, James (2005), Disarmament, Deterrence, and Denial, in: Comparative Strategy, An International Journal 24, p. 383–395.

Wittmann, Klaus (2001), The Road to NATO's New Strategic Concept, in: Schmidt, Gustav (ed.), A History of NATO. The First Fifty Years, Palgrave Macmillan: London, p. 220–237.

Wivel, Anders (2011), Security Dilemma, in: Badie, Bertrand/Berg-Schlosser, Dirk/Morlino, Leonardo (eds.), International Encyclopedia of International Science, Sage Publications: Thousand Oaks, p. 2389–2391.